Tennis
for Schools

By the same author

LIVE WITH HARCOURT ROY
(Gateway Book Co., Thorsons Publishers. 1969)

JOGGING
(Thorsons, Northants. 1969)

PHYSICAL FITNESS FOR SCHOOLS
(Pelham Books, London 1971)

PHYSICAL FITNESS FOR BOYS
(Pelham Books, London. 1972)

SOCCER AND RUGBY TRAINING SCHEMES FOR SCHOOLS
(Schoolmaster Publishing Co. Ltd. 1972)

BEGINNER'S GUIDE TO SWIMMING AND WATER SAFETY
(Pelham Books, London. 1972)

Tennis for Schools

Harcourt Roy

Illustrations by PETER FORD

PELHAM BOOKS

First published in Great Britain by
PELHAM BOOKS LTD
52 Bedford Square,
London WC1B 3EF
1974

© 1974 by Harcourt Roy

All Rights Reserved. No part of this publication
may be reproduced, stored in a retrieval system,
or transmitted, in any form or by any means,
electronic, mechanical, photocopying, recording
or otherwise, without the prior permission
of the Copyright owner

0 7207 0610 6

Set and printed in Great Britain by
Tonbridge Printers Ltd, Peach Hall Works,
Tonbridge, Kent in Times ten on twelve point
on paper supplied by P. F. Bingham Ltd,
and bound by Dorstel Press, Harlow

Contents

Illustrations 7
Acknowledgements 9

Introduction
The Tennis Image 11
The Mental Attitude 12
From the Beginning 13
Do We Need A Reason? 14
Practical Reminders 19

Part One Beginning Regular Racket Tennis
1 The Essential Role of Biodynamics 23
2 Where and How to Start 33
3 Equipment: Rackets, Balls and Personal Gear 37
4 'Free Play', Or Direct Teaching? 45
5 The Boredom Factor 50
6 Enlarging on Practical Reminders for the Teacher 53

Part Two Grips, Footwork, Stance and Strokes
7 Difference in Basic Learning Situations 59
8 The Strokes 60

9	Stroke Play: Standard Factors	62
10	Basic Essential Grips	64
11	The 'Predator' Stance, or 'Ready' Position	70
12	Groundstrokes: Forehand and Backhand Drives	75
13	Service and Smash	87
14	Volleys and Half-volleys	104
15	The Lobs	111
16	Touch Shot Volleys: Lob, Drop, Stop	114
17	Other Specialised Touch Shots: Slice, Cut, Chop, Chip	119
18	Scrambling	123

Part Three Skills, Practices and Fitness

19	Check List of Teaching and Training Points	131
20	Sample Lesson Plan	137
21	Activities and Skills	142
22	Shadowing and Feeding	145
23	Selected Tennis Activities	151
24	Fitness	164

Part Four Helpful Comment and Information

Problems With School Tennis	179
Rules of Lawn Tennis	184
Major Competitions	194
Organisations	203
Further Reading and Teaching Material	211
Definition of a Club	218
Late News Flash! The L.T.A. Green Shield Grass Roots Coaching Scheme	220
BP International Tennis Fellowship	221
Competence or Competitiveness?	223

Illustrations

Fig.		Page
1	The Tennis Image	10
2	Without a thought for biodynamics	24
3	The 'Unicorn'	26
4	The 'Long Neck'	26
5	Faulty spinal curve and pelvic tilt	27
6	Corrected	27
7	Excessive lumbar curve and forward tilt	27
8	Corrected – 'Keep the basin full'	27
9	Reaching: stress areas due to faulty foot placement	29
10	Corrected	29
11	Plan of the courts	35
12	Practice wall	36
13	Do-it-yourself practice wall	36
14	The racket	39
15	'Shake-hands' grip	64
16	Backhand grip	66
17	Service grip – 'Chopper'	68
18	The 'Predator' Stance for receiving	72
19	(a) hitting *along* the leading leg	75
	(b) hitting *across* the leading leg	75
20	Back-swing, pivot and place – *Forehand Drive*	76
21	Weight transfer, anchor and forward stroke	77
22	Watch and strike	78
23	Watch and follow-through	79
24	Pivot and place	80

25	Back-swing, pivot and place – *Backhand Drive*	83
26	Weight transfer, anchor and forward stroke	84
27	Watch and strike	85
28	Watch and follow-through	86
29	Placing the ball – *Beginners' Service*	89
30	Simple 'Shoulder Serve'	90
31	'Shoulder Serve' progression	91
32	Service stance and 'Pendulum' swing – *Full Service*	93
33	Placing the ball and backswing	94
34	'Throwing' the racket head at the ball	95
35	Follow-through and stepping forward	96
36	Placing the ball for the 'slice', 'cannonball' and 'kicker'	97
37	Long contact	99
38	Getting set for the 'Smash'	101
39	Special stance for the 'Backhand Smash'	102
40	The 'Forehand Volley'	105
41	The 'Backhand Volley'	106
42	The 'Half-volley'	107
43	Scrambling for difficult shots	126
44	Padder-tennis	160
45	Personal fitness training for tennis	173

Acknowledgements

It was good to have the encouragement and support of the major tennis organisations across the English-speaking countries when collecting the material for this book. These four were a great help: The Lawn Tennis Association, with its headquarters in London and its official monthly magazine – *Lawn Tennis;* The Lawn Tennis Foundation of Great Britain; the United States Lawn Tennis Association, and The Lawn Tennis Association of Australia. What was particularly helpful was their willingness and readiness to reply to enquiry and investigation with charming courtesy and practical information and advice.

It is sincerity like this that gives a writer an enormous boost, confirming his initial belief that the project was infinitely worthwhile. It certainly strengthens his conviction that tennis deserves and is going to get increasing status and support in most countries across the world, with promotion of the game for youth a leading priority everywhere. This is the whole point of bringing out this book now. Here's to tennis – The best family sport in the world with the biggest age range!

Slazengers Ltd., leading manufacturers in the tennis business, were naturally helpful and responsive to enquiry. I'm glad of their mutual interest in this project and for their support of the art work in particular. Their practical help is much appreciated.

H.R.

Fig. 1. THE TENNIS IMAGE
To be seen and felt

Introduction

The Tennis Image

An experience to be admired by the observer, thoroughly enjoyed by the performer and which gives much pleasure to both. A powerful stimulant and motivation for the player – how he feels in action: 'This is me and it's wonderfully pleasing.'

* The lithe, 'predator' stance.
* The relaxed alertness and keen eye.
* The quick, pantherish reaction and smooth, attractive movement.
* The 'Unicorn' posture: leading the movement with the brow and freeing the neck vertebrae from constriction and tension.
* The comfortably spaced feet and slightly flexed knees for balance and control. The 'spring-kneed' readiness.
* The sense of powerful springing in the legs.
* The feeling of the racket being a natural extension of the arm as it strokes, punches and smashes.
* The role of the non-racket arm for light finger support, sighting, balance and control.
* The superb confidence of smooth, fluent stroking.
* The general impression of controlled power and velocity.
* The deceptive impression of simplicity and ease.
* The relentless, driving energy and will to win.

Introduction

The Mental Attitude

It is best that pupils catch on from the beginning to what is being undertaken when they elect for tennis. These points can help newcomers to start off with the right idea and allow them ample time for consideration about the seriousness (or otherwise) of their approach to the game. But if in doubt, they can be reassured; a serious approach need not reduce the fun and light-hearted enjoyment, which is always available. Serious intention will increase the respect, the desire to learn and the rewards of personal improvement – fast.

* The mental attitude towards this sport can be an indication of innate intelligence. It is revealing of the inner self. How is the pupil shaping-up to the special and exacting demands of tennis?

* Pupils should be encouraged to see tennis as an important major sport. It should never be treated as a minor, 'filler' activity, but given equal status with any of the major seasonal sports.

* Tennis has one big feature in its favour: it need not be restricted as a seasonal sport at all. This gives it the extra dimension of a serious pupil-sport relationship.

* There is a decided matching of wits at a close, personal level, demanding trained self-discipline and sportsmanship.

* Players must be ready and willing to be alert, keen with anticipation, sharp in response, aggressive in attack, unshaken in defence and courteous to their partners and opponents at all times.

* Good manners and courtesy to a partner and opponent alike is of vital importance and an integral part of the game.

* Laziness is a luxury that cannot be afforded in tennis. Idlers are alien.

* Players should at all times care enough about what they are doing to make the effort and play their best. If they do they will be greatly admired, highly respected – and enjoy repeated invitations to play.

Introduction

I wouldn't want this to appear too idealistic, but a weakness of mine is having an exuberance of good faith in the young. I have this feeling that if they are given a strong lead, meaning something good and useful, a large percentage of them will respond.

With tennis, we can offer them a lively, fun-type game with an attractive social value and practical fitness effect. They can observe this effect on the lithe, sun-bronzed bodies of the international players. We shouldn't need to be salesmen on this score, tennis is a game our pupils should want readily once their appetite is whetted. What I am concerned about, however, is seeing that they take to the game in an eager, spirited fashion, backed by the right intentions. They should want to see themselves improve as worthy of the game.

However, any activity can be spolit by over-selling the keenness and enthusiasm to dilettante customers, who never pretended to enjoy an equal interest and participation in the first place. So if tennis matters enormously to one group, we must allow that a similar response may not be matched by others. In their case, they may never progress beyond using tennis as a temporary stop-gap between more serious leisure activities of their choice. They simply may not want to improve, nor see any reason to do so. In fact, their version of tennis may never advance to mean anything more than merely a Sunday morning knock-up before lunch.

Part of our teaching will be in knowing what line to take and how far to go in our promotion of tennis for the masses. Along with this, there will be constant self-critical review of our method of presentation and its effect on the recruitment to the game.

From the Beginning

Tennis developed from Handball, a very old game, of which Irish Handball is most popular and was first played in France about six hundred years ago. It was usually played indoors. This old kind of tennis is now called real (meaning royal) tennis. There are still a few real tennis courts in Europe. The first lawn tennis club was formed in England in 1872 and the first Wimbledon championship was played five years later.

The aim of the game is to hit the ball over the net and into your opponent's court. If he misses, or returns into the net or

Introduction

outside your court, you win the rally. A rally is a series of strokes leading to one point being scored.

A game begins with one player serving. If his opponent fails to return the ball over the net after one bounce or misses it altogether, the server wins the point. The score is 15-love. If he continues to win points, the score progresses to 30-love, 40-love, and then game. If the opposing player wins the same number of rallies the score will go 15-all, 30-all, and 40-all (usually called deuce). At deuce, one player must win two rallies in succession to win the game. The first player to win six games wins the set, providing he is two games ahead at the end.

At the end of each set the player who has been serving becomes the receiver. The first player to win two sets in a three-set match, or three sets if it is a five-set match, is the match winner.

One modern development has been the use of the so-called tie-breaker to decide a set. When the score in games is six-all, each player has two serves in succession. The first player to be in the lead by two clear points wins the set. The system is not used in the last set of a match.

The four main championships of international tennis are the Australian, French, American, and English (Wimbledon).

Do We Need a Reason

Fun, Fame or Fortune?

Do many children wonder about joining First Division soccer clubs, becoming Olympic swimmers, or playing on the Centre Court at Wimbledon? Is this a legitimate incentive for them?

Games teachers may dismiss such motivation as unrealistic. Coaching their pupils towards such heights in the world of sport is not how teachers see their job. And, more likely, there is neither sufficient time nor space with the over-large classes they get.

But they do see themselves, primarily, as introducing exciting activities, stimulating sporting appetites, teaching fundamentals, encouraging and developing ability and skills, improving fitness and performance and promoting healthy and continuing fun and enjoyment. Basically, they wish to provide opportunity and pro-

Introduction

mote the pleasure of participation in a wide variety of sports, ultimately of the pupils' own choice.

Tennis most certainly must be one of them, of *equal importance* to the pupil and the school as soccer, rugby, hockey, athletics and swimming. This may be dependent upon whether or not the staff includes a tennis enthusiast keen to transmit this to the children.

So the school has this imaginative physical education programme of preparing pupils for fitness and active recreation, as an antidote to the hazard of becoming inactive, unfit citizens in an increasingly mechanised society. If there are potential champions in the P.E. classes, no doubt they will emerge – with suitable encouragement and training. The child with a quick eye, sharp reflexes and natural athletic ability will always be recognised and respected – but what about the mainstream of mediocre performers?

This is the clue to the main purpose of this book. It is not exclusively for the child prodigy, or for the specialist player aiming for the top competitive leagues, even though it would be nice to think it might help along that road, too. I'm sure it can.

The aim is to stimulate masses of youthful appetites for tennis and help teach the basics to start playing it reasonably well, because of what tennis has to offer, physically and socially, as an active personal sport. Advanced performance and top competitive abilitity can develop, if it is wanted. I hope it is.

Everyone Enjoys Hitting a Ball

As a form of psycho-physical release it is positively therapeutic, as well as being great fun, of course. Apart from that, anyone who introduces tennis (or any sport) has the responsibility and probably the compulsion too for improving their pupil's playing ability. Even the coach needs fulfilment!

So I'm offering this for dual purpose: for the teacher or games coach to use with training sessions; and also to help the non-performer, or raw beginner direct, as a personal coaching manual. To help them to discover personally the thrill and enjoyment to be extracted from the physical movement and challenge of hitting a tennis ball – to a partner during practice or opponent in a game, or simply against a practice wall.

The idea is to quickly learn to do it well enough to gain real

Introduction

pleasure and satisfaction (both coaching and learning). And this skill has to be felt and enjoyed *within* the performer, and recognised and appreciated by the observer.

This is not as over-simplified as it might seem to some stale players or hardened coaches. The dynamic, lively-minded ones, for example, know that there is never any such person as a perfect player, and no top limit to perfection. Once started as a player, *the learning process never stops* No one knows it all. This is their constant incentive for self-improvement and a continuous source of pleasure. It is self-induced, and self-perpetuating – apart from a little vital stimulation from the coach, now and then!

Endless 'Learner' Material

For every retiring tennis-pensioner, there are scores of emerging children with a latent desire and the potential ability to discover for themselves the pleasure that awaits them on a tennis court.

Tennis For Schools emphasises that this pleasure of participation is to be gained from both the lesser-known padder-tennis (see page 34), as well as from the hard-core tennis of the Wimbledon and Davis Cup championships. (Sorry, why not the local tennis club too? Or the school club itself?)

The basic requirement, at practically any age, is that the performer should get a rewarding thrill from hitting the ball with satisfying control and pleasing accuracy. There is this enormous personal satisfaction to be savoured from stroking, tickling, chopping, punching, slicing, spinning, driving or power-smashing a tennis-ball with a racket or a padder-bat. It releases that inner fulfilment that we can feel doing us so much good. It always has for me. Passing some of this on to the kids seems fair enough.

This is what we are promoting. Call it 'Tennis for the masses' if you like. The more young people introduced to it the better. Why shouldn't it achieve the general popularity of hop-scotch or park football, and then be developed from there? The biggest difficulty that tennis has to overcome is the insufficiency of playing areas combined with lack of competent coaches and really interested teachers for mass or class instruction.

And here's where padder-tennis, appropriately modified, can help overcome even this common handicap. It is ideal for the school playground, back-yard, street, cul-de-sac, front lawn or

Introduction

holiday promenade. Then whenever the desire and the muscles are strong enough, there's always the fun and sociability of the local tennis club or public courts to encourage the conversion to racket tennis and improved performance (if the school hasn't done this already, which it should, from the primary years).

Please: Equal Ranking, Status and Enthusiasm

I've seen many children neglected during games periods (I won't call them 'lessons'). The selected and the vigorous ones are taken and coached (or sometimes just taken!) on the hockey or the soccer pitch, or in the cricket nets. The dumplings, the dimwits (forgive me), the weaklings and the anti-body-contact types and the ones without games kit are left to amuse themselves on the tennis courts and the padder-tennis areas as best they can, without instruction. I expect you're familiar with some of the 'convincing' arguments proffered for this procedure!

This form of neglect doesn't do the tennis image (or the equipment) any good, reducing it to the the lowered level of a second-class, substitute play activity, a filler (and tennis isn't the only activity used as this form of 'convenience'!) In this context it is used just to keep a few awkward kids occupied, without even a pretence of teaching. Of course, it may well suit those few anti-physical types, left alone to play pit-pat in a desultory fashion and work out their own energy-expenditure, until their deficient interest evaporates completely, which doesn't take long! Then from awkward kids, they can become problem kids. They're also the chief sufferers.

Meanwhile, how can tennis be expected to enjoy equal status with its major team game rivals? Can it attract massive support of enthusiastic participants, at all levels of ability, all genuinely keen on improving their performance for fun and fitness, all reading and *feeling their stroke-play within themselves w*ith keen pleasure? Oh, I'm sure we can give it a good boost in the right direction through our P.E. classes and try to correct the imbalance. But we shall certainly need greater practical support from all the education and local authorities in providing very many more practice and playing areas, in schools, youth clubs and the public arena, indoor and out. Meanwhile, we can improvise, just to get it started and introduced, at least.

Introduction

And when we feel we need a little extra practical help, we've only got to drop a line to The Lawn Tennis Foundation of Great Britain, The Queen's Club, West Kensington, London, W.14. Tel: 01-385 4233/4). Tell them what we're trying to do – and they'll be delighted to assist in many ways. It's lovely to have the comforting support of a practical organisation like this backing you up. Try it!

Postscript

I wouldn't want what I've written so far to be misconstrued as merely light-hearted, inconsequential fun and games, over-emphasising 'fun' and 'pleasure' and ignoring hard training, sweat and fitness. No one is going to escape entirely from this, don't worry.

We know these aspects of any sport must go hand-in-hand as an inseparable whole. A person can gain enormous pleasure from applying him or herself to serious skill-training and physical conditioning, with suitable encouragement. This is all part of the essential grasp of the sport. In our case, tennis. Our kids should see (or read about) what the top pros do to stay on top! They still enjoy playing.

What I want to do is to be realistic. I'm not aiming to discover, train and condition tennis athletes for the Big Time international circuits, but to encourage the maximum number of boys and girls, through their schools and clubs, to become actively interested in playing tennis as their choice of leisure time sport – for life. This is where the real value lies – as a fun-fitness activity, with powerful social overtones.

The rigorous, dedicated training can come. It will have to, if some of these youngsters decide to pursue competitive school, club and county tennis seriously. It depends upon how they take to the game, or even before that, how it was introduced to them, way back in the early primary school. Quite a psychological point. So much spoiling can occur at the impressionable age.

In any case, once past the purely 'fun and games' stage, the persuasion for improved fitness will be coming through firmly. In fact, it's absolutely essential for anyone with any self-respect who sees himself wedded to the racket; for this is what it means to any young man or woman wanting to make more than a fair showing at tennis as their major sport. They've got to get it in their blood, wrap themselves around it, take it into themselves.

I love to see the public courts during summer evenings and at weekends, alive with enthusiastic young people in white sports gear contrasting attractively with sun-tanned skin, applying themselves with eager concentration to improving their tennis – and delighting each other. They are invariably, happy, healthy youngsters (regardless of age!). Somehow, this is what it's all about – getting as many recruits as we can to see it this way.

Practical Reminders

1. Teacher or coach? How do you see the difference?
2. Develop and maintain a two-way relationship of mutual confidence.
3. Variety in teaching and practice – essential.
4. Plan for maximum pupil participation.
5. Necessary to achieve minimum inactivity or idleness by pupils.
6. Aim for a high level of personal example.
7. Considerate and advantageous positioning of class and teacher.
8. Careful lesson planning for maximum effective use of equipment, space and personnel.
9. Encourage pupil initiative, co-operation and self-directed discipline.
10. Development of most effective class teaching procedure.
11. Ways of incorporating individual attention and coaching into the class situation.
12. A progress record by 'log book' or card system recommended.

Part One

Beginning Regular Racket Tennis

Once the feel of that racket has been impressed on the muscles of the striking arm, and its action imprinted on the nerve paths, the player seldom escapes from the experience. He doesn't want to. The sensation is too pleasurable.

1

The Essential Role of Biodynamics

'Biodynamics' refers to the forces interacting within the body, concerning the nervous system and motor muscles controlling dynamic posture and movement. The effect on the human body is physical beauty, grace and harmony with natural, attractive movers. Persons trained to use their mechanism correctly in action include gymnasts, divers and dancers. But the large majority of people, children included, by their habitual lack of awareness about posture and movement, are destined to emerge as 'normal' – with malfunctioning, physical distortion and permanent growth and posture defects. This is not covered by conventional posture training in schools.

The outcome is that, by the day-by-day, habitually recurring faulty movements and postures of home, school, office and factory, unnecessary stress and fatigue are created and occupational and industrial efficiency reduced. Also, because of this faulty use generally, the performance of children and adults at games and sports is likewise impaired. This is where a tennis coach would be most concerned to bring about their improved performance by the principles of biodynamics as they relate to the good management of the body. It is conceivable that a process of *physical re-education* would go hand-in-hand with the new experience of tennis instruction.

Unfortunately, the child acquires its bad habits of posture and movement early in his development, by actions performed repeatedly in the wrong way, without correction by the adult in charge. As skills of correct body mechanics and use are seldom acquired as a birthright, they should be taught with as much importance as any other subject. It could be done in tennis. If this is approached on the basis that every move a person makes or posture he adopts is involved with biodynamics, then it can quickly become part of a person's conscious life-style for improved health and increased effectiveness for both work and sport.

Tennis for Schools

However, if you are generally aware of yourself in action – or simply occupying space, then you are likely to get the feel of biodynamic forces throughout your body, frequently. This usually can be most pleasurable, but sometimes disconcerting, depending upon their application and how you see yourself.

But whether or not a person is aware of these forces in action does affect two processes:

(1) the effect of their conscious application upon the actual movement and deployment of the person's body.

(2) the transmission of these forces through the racket, bat, club, vaulting-pole, billiard cue, bow and arrow, skates, skis or boots in use at the time – and the result experienced from using this equipment.

The basic hazard of being *unaware* of these forces is that bodily malfunctioning and movement distortion can occur without the 'conscious control of the individual' (a biodynamic term). Consequently, the person's games' skill and ability suffers, a reason for us to include this study with our work on tennis.

Biodynamics, body-shape and function

'*The shape of the body is the sum of its everyday movements*' This is the principle to keep floating about in our minds and apply to our own, personal movement-patterns. The functioning of our motor-muscles and subsequent body-shape is largely determined by what we have done with this anatomical structure ever since we started kicking in the cot. We are, generally, the

Fig. 2. Without a thought for biodynamics

The Essential Role of Biodynamics

unconscious sculptor of our living clay (some folk may be aware of what they are doing; but not many).

Look around at the crowds in the supermarkets next time you go shopping and the evidence will be clear. It won't be complimentary to the human race.

The two basic factors that decide just how (or if) we apply this principle are – ARE WE AWARE? and DO WE CARE?

Because of daily, habitual, malfunctioning, ill-considered movement and repeated habit-patterns of faulty and stressful posture, we unthinkingly mould ourselves from near-perfect seedlings into ugly misshapen growths. We have to consider what effect this habitual faulty and stressful way of moving has on our tennis. It's not much good going to the bother of trying to correct footwork, stance and strokes, if at the same time we are grossly ignorant of biodynamics in the way we move generally. This unawareness simply makes the physical learning process in tennis very much harder and the unconscious development of faults that much easier.

So the case is put here for biodynamics to be included in all schools' physical education and made a special part of tennis instruction in particular.

Key Anatomical points linked with Biodynamics

HEAD – NECK – SHOULDERS – ABDOMEN – PELVIS – KNEES – FEET

Of these seven, three crucial regions exert a dominating influence on human posture and movement: (1) *head-neck relationship* (the 'Unicorn Posture'), (2) *abdominal-pelvic relationship* (the 'Centre Control') and (3) *leg and foot placement* (the 'Foot-Forward Principle').

(1) The 'Unicorn Posture' and the 'Long Neck'. The head-neck relationship is the vital control area determining the reflex action, the direction and subsequent plane of movement – and any side-effects. Think of what this can do to tennis.

The golfer, tennis-player, rugby player kicking a goal, ballet dancer spinning superbly, the falling cat which lands on its feet, acrobat, gymnast, high diver and trampoline tumbler – all apply this head-neck relationship, principally, the head *leading the*

Tennis for Schools

movement. Visualise and feel it as LEADING WITH THE BROW.

If they don't already know it instinctively like the cat, they must all learn the importance of head placement in initiating and guiding the direction and the follow-through pattern of their performance.

With everyday movements too, in straight, functional living, this head-control principle affects all activities. For example: in a rising turn from a chair, in emerging from a car, in putting on a top-coat or jacket, in ascending stairs – whatever the action, there is need for conscious head-control *at the commencement* of the intended movement or posture.

Omit this initial control and the resultant action can cause constriction, stress and tension in the neck, malfunction and the awkward, ungraceful placement of the limbs and body. Again, think how this influences your tennis.

   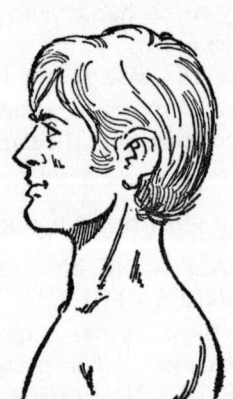

Fig. 3. The 'Unicorn'   Fig. 4. The 'Long Neck'

Explaining how it's done

To feel within our head-neck relationship that we are 'pointing the unicorn's horn' and 'making a long neck', we must picture in our mind's eye the spiralling horn emerging from our hairline the brow. Visualise too, carrying it poised forward, with the jaw held down, in the manner of the spirited Arabian stallion.

Drop the chin and stretch the back of the neck, feeling the stretch of the muscles from the base of the skull to the shoulders.

Then draw back the head to an easy, vertical balance. But it is *draw back,* not bend. This is 'making a long neck' and it frees constricting tension, the opposite from the retracted and constricted neck. But don't tense the throat.

Former years of incorrect postural habit may well restrict this action, making it seem difficult, even unnatural. Physical assistance from a partner's hands to guide this head-neck position is

Fig. 5. Faulty spinal curve and pelvic tilt

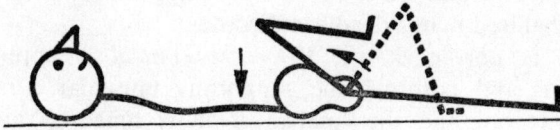

Fig. 6. Corrected

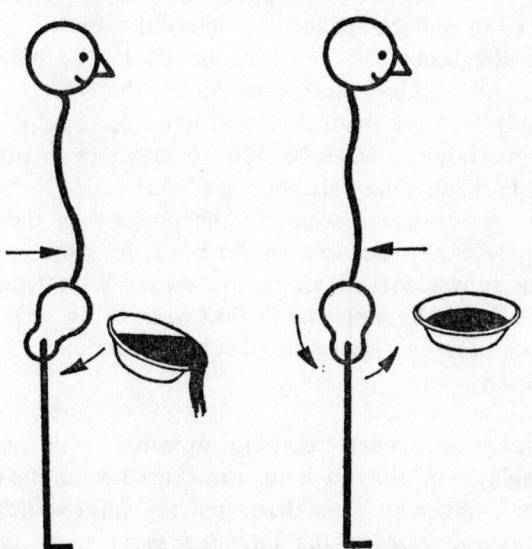

Fig. 7. Excessive lumbar curve and forward tilt

Fig. 8. Corrected 'Keep the basin full'

advisable. Then your own self-instruction with the aid of two mirrors can complete this re-education of that vital region.

(2) *The 'Centre Control.* The abdomen, sometimes called the 'second spine', and the pelvis, with its related muscles, jointly provide the foundation for body movement. Around this key point is wrapped the great muscular corset, designed to keep the soft vunerable tissues and vital organs safely in place. It is here that the most powerful muscles are attached, and from here the magnificient spinal column rises as a pedestal for the brain.

But much misuse and distortion is initiated in this region. Prolonged, slumped sitting, too many unrelieved hours at desk, TV set or steering-wheel, and habitually allowing a distended gut to push outwards against the waistband will soften and weaken this natural muscular corset. This is the atrophy of disuse. Mechanised man's deadliest disorder.

But it is not inevitable. If *centre control* is applied in all movements and postures, the supporting muscular corset of the abdominal wall and the lumbar spine is toned-up and strengthened naturally as you sit, stand and move, just as it is with animals. This is the natural benefit of biodynamics and to a large extent can replace artificially contrived exercise.

'Keeping the basin full' must be linked in the mind with all movements and postures, until maintaining the correct strengthening pelvic tilt becomes instinctive and natural. It helps to remember that you should always be able to insert, with no difficulty, two fingers between your waistband and you!

(3) *The 'Foot-Forward Principle'.* The position of the feet, their relationship to each other and to the body, initially, helps control and correct movement all along the spine. With tennis in particular, this is vitally important. But with living generally, four dynamic postures are involved: reaching, bending, stooping and pushing. Briefly . . .

a. Reaching: whenever reaching upwards with one or two arms, (hanging out the washing, drawing the curtains, reaching a high shelf, brushing your hair, playing an overhead shot in tennis . . .) *before starting the intended movement, advance one foot comfortably in front of the other..* 'Placing your best foot forward'.

The Essential Role of Biodynamics

b. Bending: whenever you have cause to bend or lean forward, (over baby's cot, the filing cabinet, a low table, a rose bush, playing leap-frog...) *place one foot forward first.*

c. Stooping: when you stoop, (gardening, to swob the lino, pick up an object, to speak to a small child...) *before you bend your knees advance one foot forward* (on occasions, to squat is better).

d. 'Pushing: when about to push against a heavy or resistant object (an immobile car or a stubborn elephant...); or in any situation which requires you to lean your weight inwards, do it with *one foot forward.* This will avoid the common error and strain of pushing with the belly.

Fig. 9. Reaching: stress areas due to faulty foot placement

Fig. 10. Corrected

FOOT-FORWARD: SUMMARY OF BASIC POINTS

Reaching forwards and upwards – bending or stooping downwards – sitting down – rising from a chair or seat – pushing against a weighty or resistant object – shooting a bow – forehand, backhand, service and smash strokes in racket games.

Recognising and applying these forces to tennis

The biodynamics of tennis ought not to be ignored. It frequently is. But I'm sure this is not a calculated, deliberate act of neglect. The difficulty is two-fold:

(1) Firstly, the number of coaches and players who genuinely have never considered applying biodynamics to tennis, is large. This form of dynamic study hasn't been part of their instruction. It could be.

(2) Secondly, the aim is to achieve a fine balance: between ignoring the biodynamics of human movement altogether, and including its study to the point of complexity and exasperation. Both extremes are to be avoided.

Perhaps this latter reaction produces the same result anyway – possibly a deliberate overlooking or setting aside of this essential movement study in tennis.

So, we recognise and embrace the study of biodynamics, not pretend it doesn't exist. It can be less difficult than we might imagine. To guarantee success, we have only to avoid complexity and complication. Then we stand a good chance of not becoming exasperated quickly and reject the study angrily. We can't afford to!

Fortunately, we have the perfect set-up with tennis – to start simply at the beginning – with the *basic position of readiness* we adopt before, between and after strokes and play – the 'Predator' Stance. We'll be coming to this again shortly.

Key Words and Phrases used in Biodynamics

* Use of the self.
* The 'Unicorn' posture.
* Lead with the brow
* 'Foot forward principle'.

* Keep the basin full.
* Pelvic tilt.
* Conscious control of the individual.
* Head-neck relationship.
* Occupying space gracefully.
* Secret of 'Centre Control'.
* Making a 'long neck'.
* The 'five-second transformation'.
* The 'broken line of ugliness'.
* The 'vertical line of beauty'.
* 'Four-point Sag'.
* End-gaining.

The idea is, to follow this brief introduction by an enjoyable study of *The Alexander Principle* by Dr Wilfred Barlow (Victor Gollancz, London. 1973. £3.00). And then apply its teachings to the stance, footwork and movements of tennis for improved performance.

Further reading and study:

Live With Harcourt Roy. A modern, realistic and practical approach to health, fitness and vitality (Thorsons Publishers Ltd., Denington Estate, Wellingborough, Northants).
Physical Fitness For Schools 1971. £2 and *Physical Fitness For Boys* 1972. £1.90. Both by Harcourt Roy (Pelham Books, London).
Choice of Habit: Poise, Free Movement and the Practical use of the Body by Jack Vinten Fenton (Macdonald and Evans, London. 1973). £1.25.

Postscript on Biodynamics – meaniningful points

Awareness and practice of biodynamics applies to all sports, but tennis grabs a big slice of attention for itself. Two biodynamic principles are dominant:

1 The FOOT-FORWARD PRINCIPLE
2 The BALANCED RESTING STATE

Tennis for Schools

1 The Foot-forward Principle becomes an essential, functional characteristic of stroke-play, low shots and Scrambling in particular. The appropriate foot leads the action, steps in, establishes balance, direction and body-control and provides that necessary, resilient foundation.

Without this vital principle of hitting either *along*, or *across* the *leading* leg, stroke production would be as wild and uncontrolled as incoherent speech.

PLACING THE FOOT PLACES THE PLAYER IN CHARGE

2 The Balanced Resting State of the bent knees ready position ('Predator' Stance), provides the essential mental-physical equilibrium necessary for gathering the body into attack, or defence.

It provides opportunity for frequent checking of all the key anatomical areas during brief pauses in action:

HEAD-NECK, BACK, PELVIS, KNEES, ANKLES, FEET

The total body is never completely stationary, but functioning under this principle is constantly responding to nervous stimuli and readjustment of muscle-tone in a condition of relaxed alertness, poise and balance.

This is the *Balanced Resting State;* but ideally, continually receptive to incoming stimuli, to be triggered into instant, pantherish action. Most wild-life retains this dynamic quality for survival. Man appears to have lost his through generations of urbanised, mechanised living. It will repay tennis players to regain it.

NOTE: running the rule over oneself this way, is part of the *Biodynamic Principle* to develop heightened, personal awareness and so reduce the common occurrence of bodily mis-use and malfunctioning, together with inefficient and damaging management of the body in work, sport, fitness training, and recreational activities of all kinds.

No sport and no one is beyond possibility of involvement in this form of mis-use. Awareness and practise of biodynamics in human movement, can be a form of *prevention* of malfunctioning instead of delayed 'cure'.

2

Where and How to Start

School's the place

As this is a book primarily for school use (although there's nothing to stop the individual beginner from using it), it is geared from the teacher's point of view, and also for the P.E. and games department in particular. So it is not exclusively just a coaching manual. This shouldn't deter others. They'll still extract a wealth of personal, practical information to start them on the right lines and improve their play, school or not! A tremendous amount of learning is done in a person's own time.

We must think of this sport beginning at the earliest school age – well, almost. Certainly the knowledge and the feel of it should be implanted at the Primary level, even as young as 6 years, with lighter rackets. And this is where padder tennis is so useful as a starter. We'll be coming to that in Part Three. The reason why I'm dealing with racket tennis first, is because it's the up-and-up major game with world-wide appeal, it's continuously in the public eye, and because, no doubt, many secondary school teachers and would-be players are simply tremendously keen to get on with it.

If you are of the other school, working with the younger children, let's hope this first part will be just as stimulating and useful for you. Then there's nothing to stop you switching over to the padder section and applying it to your youngsters, as well as introducing modified racket tennis. They should love it.

Persuading the boss

Equipment costs money, so you may have to persuade the Head or Principal to release some, maybe even a little extra. If there's resistance here it won't be because the Head is against tennis; but because he has weighed up the number of pupils that can

Tennis for Schools

be accommodated in a game compared with the largish financial outlay. He probably considers this unbalanced. Not like football, which can occupy a whole class for the price of one ball! Or so he may imagine. He'd be wrong anyway. We know that.

Here's a suggestion: photostat one or two pertinent passages from this book strongly emphasising the *educational* aspects of the game: courtesy and good manners, fair play and honesty (scoring), bodily awareness, desire for fitness, strong social value of mixed games, introduction to after-school tennis clubs, and so on. Ask him to kindly read them when he has a moment.

Point out that expensive outlay on hard courts is unnecessary at first. With the co-operation of the groundsman, temporary courts can be prepared and marked-out (as many as will fit) on the grass sports field for the summer term, disregarding the weather if you can. If this doesn't do the trick, the Lawn Tennis Foundation's booklet for beginners, *Let's Play Tennis*, should clinch it.

If the Head is still unmoved, then you'll have to win him over to padder tennis in the playground at least, which in any case can be played most of the year. A strong point. This shouldn't strain his purse-strings, and you'll be getting your foot in the door as a starter. He may be persuaded (and amused) in your favour by this little section alone. Damn it all! It's not for you. It's for the kids.

The court and practice areas

Presupposing you've already figured out where the 'experimental' court(s) can fit in, and if fortunate, there may be a handy brick wall long and high enough to use for class or group wall practice. I know these can be constructed, but that would be pushing your luck at this stage! Refer to our 'Problems With School Tennis' in Part Four for a few more pointers.

Meanwhile, here's the court measurements. This is what the groundsman or schoolkeeper will need. On the other hand, if there's room in the playground or sports hall for a hardcourt, then you would be better off getting it marked out professionally by contract. Your local architect's office, or Parks Department should have these services on file – they may even pay for them! The less you dig into school funds the better – for these prelimi-

Where and How to Start

naries. Although it might depend upon how quickly you want the job done. Educational departments can be terribly long-winded in making decisions where money is concerned – public money. Whereas a little ready cash at the school can get immediate action. I think you're going to have to be a convincing talker, full of persuasive conviction. A real good teacher, in fact!

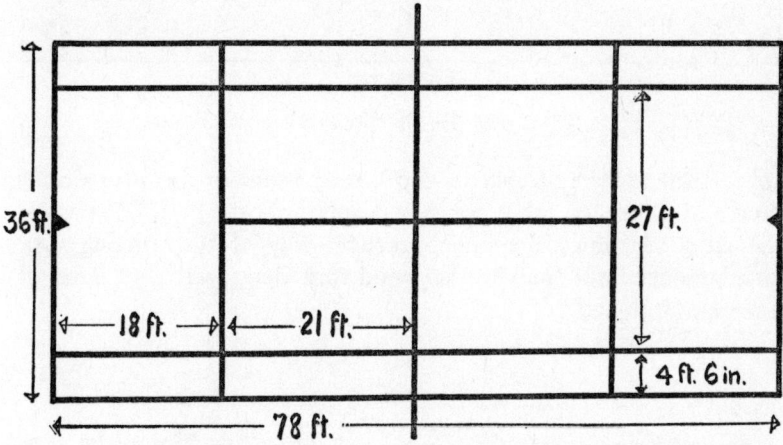

Fig. 11. PLAN OF THE COURTS (See Rules 1 and 32)

If your school hasn't had tennis before, keep pushing for the construction of permanent hard courts with all the tenacity you can muster – while you're using your temporary grass courts as action adverts. Never be deterred by the first, second or third refusal. Be sympathetic for the Head's concern about expense; but having made tennis an integral part of your P.E. programme by improvising on playing and practice areas (football field, playground, sports hall, gymnasium, and of course the nearest public courts, parks or sports centre), keep him aware that you need courts on the school grounds. Make it easier for him by doing all the preliminary research and admin work. Show him you're the expert.

Back to wall practice again. This really is essential. You'll be lucky if you have a long, high wall handy; but there's bound to be smaller brick or stone areas, reinforced garage doors (if permitted), perhaps an extra heavy-gauge, strong boundary fence. You'll need a flair for improvisation and opportunism, but you'll

Tennis for Schools

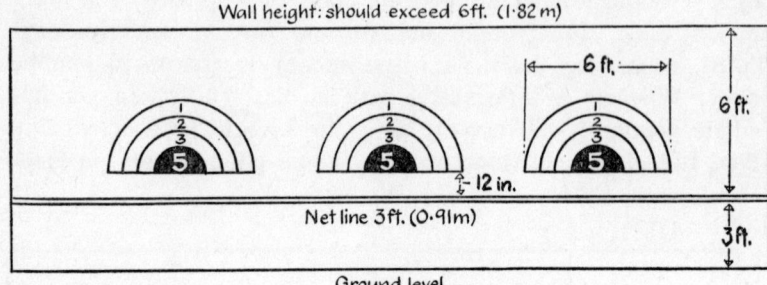

Fig. 12. Practice wall

be rewarded. Don't forget to check on permission before painting lines and targets on other people's property.

Figure 13 shows a simple, practical way of constructing your own practice wall (maybe the woodwork dept. will take it on as a working project).

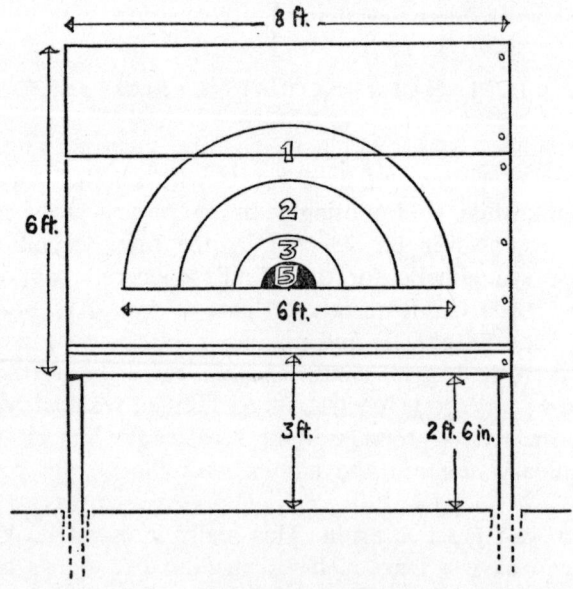

Fig. 13. Do-it-yourself practice wall

This leads us naturally to the playing equipment.

3

Equipment: Rackets, Balls and Personal Gear

Apart from obtaining all the equipment you need through the school funds, there is the information and advice to be passed on to pupils to help them kit themselves out properly, should they wish to take up the game in their own time. Without this help, they can be misled by outside influences. But this applies to most sports and to all consumer goods.

Choosing the Right Racket

As the racket has to be a natural extension of the striking arm, the size, weight and feel of it must be exactly right for the individual.

Here's where you must discourage pupils from accepting hand-me-downs. Friends and relations who imagine they are doing the youngster a service by handing on their old racket, are in fact doing the young beginner a disservice at a most crucial age. The weight, size of grip and balance is generally wrong for the immature, untrained muscles, and the stringing has often slackened off badly causing young players to slash or overstrike to gain the power they think they want.

Offer professional advice to those pupils interested enough to buy their own rackets, before they put down their money. For young children, a *full-sized* but *lighter* racket is better for their development than the so-called 'junior' racket, which is heavy in the head and unbalanced, with its shorter, thinner handle.

The age level for starting with this full-size light racket can be 10 years. Below this age, the racket could be too long and scrape the ground, plus encouraging the fault common to weak-wristed players of dropping the racket head to lift the ball over the net.

Tennis for Schools

School rackets

As these are bought in lots of maybe a dozen or more at a time, individual, personalised selection suffers. So you do the next best thing and group your purchases into assorted sizes, thinking of the large age and size range in your classes throughout the school, from the first year to the Sixth Formers.

Racket firms are educating the buying public towards a familiarity with these size and weight classifications:

RACKET SELECTION GUIDE

CHILDREN (10 YEARS PLUS) TO ADULT

Class	WEIGHT British	WEIGHT Metric	No.	SIZE (grip) British	SIZE (grip) Metric
Extra light	12–12½ oz.	340–354g.	1	4 in.	10.2 cm
Light	12½–13 oz.	354–369g.	2	4¼ in.	10.8 cm
Light medium	13–13½ oz.	369–383g.	3	4⅜ in.	11.1 cm
Medium	13½–14 oz.	383–397g.	4	4½ in.	11.4 cm
Heavy	14 + oz.	397 + g.	5	4⅝ in.	11.7 cm
Extra heavy (made only to order)	15 oz.	425g.	6	4¾ in.	12.1 cm

As the selection and use of a racket is a very personal affair, these size-weight variations are dependent upon individual feel and comfort, initially. Changes can be made as playing style and preference emerges.

But with classes of children, the best you can do is provide a wide selection and have the pupils choose their racket by what feels comfortable and right for them. Some practical tips:

* A heavy-headed racket is unsuitable for weak wrists.

Equipment: Rackets, Balls and Personal Gear

* Spiral *nylon* stringing is recommended for extra durability under rougher conditions. e.g. the raw beginners.

* Avoid hyper-tense strings that have a hard, board effect. This reduces length of contact between ball and strings and upsets ball control with beginners. It's not all that wonderful for anyone else.

* Slacker stringing gives better touch, feel and control. (Tighter for extra power). But don't imagine I'm recommending a fishing net!

* Try different stringing before making a final choice. Certainly discuss it with someone in the know who can pass on the benefit of experience.

* *Gut* (best natural) is best for elasticity and responsiveness, possibly for the better senior players. Have some of these better quality rackets – but keep them under strict care.

* Small grip gives more wrist flexibility and velocity to the shot; larger grip gives more firmness and support.

* Storage temperature should be moderate and consistent to avoid warping of the racket head. Check the location of heating pipes, gas or electric heaters, then stack the rackets well away from them.

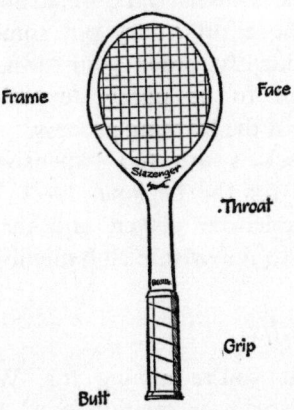

Fig. 14. The racket

Tennis for Schools

* For regular school use it would seem superfluous to include a press for each racket. Being realistic, it might be highly impracticable to expect the storekeeper (or a variety of teachers) to press up each racket accurately after use every day. You know what failings we humans have. But how about using presses for the very best rackets?

* As they are put away in the sports store, mark a coloured line around each handle to identify the different weights. This will simplify their subsequent issue and return.

* Another good tip is to protect the rounded end of each racket head with a quarter-circle plastic shield, which clips on quite firmly. This saves the strings from getting frayed where they emerge through the frame – especially as some children are holy terrors at scraping or bashing their racket head on the ground. Enquire from your educational supplier or local sports retailer.

CHOICE AND MAKE

This is dependent upon individual preference, compared against cost, serviceability, durability and the type of racket maintenance a firm is prepared to offer. At this level of mass supply for beginners' classes, price is probably the deciding factor. So obtain and study a selection of tennis catalogues, then make additional enquiries from other schools' P.E. departments and professional colleagues. Make the effort to try out some of their gear. Only then can you confidently order your own. Even so, your first order may turn out to be purely 'experimental'. This is fair enough. It's all part of the learning process.

Metal framed rackets are too expensive for general school use, and unsuitable for the beginner level. They are more suited to the skilled, experienced player, and that's the gist of it. So leave their purchase to the private club member.

Cheap, quality balls

This is really what you're aiming for. Whereas the low-price 'seconds' and similar lower quality 'new' balls can be absolute rubbish – and false economy.

Equipment: Rackets, Balls and Personal Gear

A good system is an arrangement with local clubs and tennis schools to purchase their secondhand balls, generally used for only one week. These are originally top quality, like Slazengers, but can be contracted for at about 5p each, or less; yet will retain most of their playable qualities.

This is the better method of obtaining the best ball at the cheapest price, with an excellent guarantee. You see, you're going to need so many of them – to keep the maximum number of pupils occupied, interested and learning.

Personal gear – look good, feel right

To look good and feel just right for your sport is as important as handling your racket skilfully. Clothing matters in all sports and very much so with tennis. (On a par with cricket, in fact). A clean, neat, well-dressed player indicates a clear thinker, a person who cares about what he or she is doing. A good appearance improves confidence and is the best advertisement for oneself.

Casual, spontaneous, trendy shopping for this purpose is not good enough. A little careful research is essential. So encourage pupils to go to the shop that specialises in sports clothing of the kind trademarked, which combines the qualities a player needs: attractiveness with design simplicity, functional comfort and maximum efficiency and durability.

A player needs slightly loose, comfortably-fitting shirt and shorts or skirt, that absorbs perspiration, will wash and dry easily and quickly – of drip-dry material and soft; absorbent, white socks to match foot size accurately (no guesswork here). Foot comfort and hygiene is so important for good, enjoyable tennis. Ask your sports supplier about the latest design in tennis socks.

As regards shoes: these need to be accurately fitted to correct foot size. It is equally as important to do this as with any type of shoe a person gets measured up for. Pupils must never be allowed to think that it's all right to make do with any old, ill-fitting 'gym' shoe. This is folly. So impress this principle upon them, repeatedly.

The tennis shoe itself is more serviceable and comfortable if it is of best quality, with a cushiony insole and thick, resilient, serrated rubber soles. Look for the heavy-duty, chunky style.

Tennis for Schools

Remember, they're as important to a tennis player as tyres are to a racing driver.

Underwear should be selected and reserved to go with the outer tennis-wear; never allow pupils to simply retain their every-day pants, vest and bra for playing sport in; this is a slovenly habit that you should not permit them to indulge in apart from being inefficient. Like everything else in this P.E. and games business, it's all part of the educational process.

Sorry if this seems so obvious; but getting kids to change their underwear for sport can be a difficult job, especially as they get older. You'd think they might have more sense, but the truth is many are just plain ignorant and lazy. (Not that they would admit it) Although I know this can depend so much upon their kind of home and social background. Sometimes a teacher has to be father, mother and all! It can be a rewarding job, they tell me.

So now, as regards to this personal gear: pupils must learn how essential it is to dress to suit the sport. This is basic. If it is covered by their compulsory physical education clothing while still at school, all well and good. If not, then their parents may need educating too!

Lastly, a player needs an attractive carry-all to transport his gear in, and as it is going to get some rough handling it needs to be strong. Go for the sort with reinforced seams, heavy-duty zip, and a fixed name label – a large one.

One more thing. Tennis clothing should be white. That's the way it is. This means purchased white and maintained white.

I know you'll come up against the tattered, faded jeans and pop T-shirt brigade and a variety of scruffy foot-wear. And they'll feel perfectly at home in it – that's their style. And this creates the dilemma – for you. But try to get across somehow, that it's not tennis! The point is too, they're *not* home.

In some cases there'll be the temptation to let it go. You know the sort of thing: 'If they're happy the way they are, why upset them and make it harder on ourselves by imposing our standards on them? After all, we don't want to alienate them, do we?' And so on.

In fact, they are not your standards. It's the discipline of tennis. You're just passing on the correct information as the intermediary in this case. Why should you feel insecure, nervous or apologetic for that?

This is a rot that pervades a lot of so-called teaching. A kind of fear or reluctance to promote firm standards and principles. God knows why! Although we've all met those teacher-types who imagine they'll be more 'acceptable' by pupils if they appear like them. Do they really think they're fooling the kids?

Please count me out of this form of confused thinking and muddled anarchy. It upsets me. Anyway, surely such a crazy dilemma doesn't intrude into tennis, so let's get on to some action happily.

Oh, by the way: don't we interpret and use as our ally, this 'discipline of the sport' with every activity we introduce and teach? Presumably, setting the initial personal example of dress and behaviour ourselves. Well, anything we can do to avoid comeback and criticism is only common sense and common courtesy in a way.

Another Thought

I've been commenting on equipment and personal gear in the context of school, teacher and pupils. This is why I haven't written directly to the individual player with personal suggestions, but kept in mind his place in the school group and his actual needs there.

Nevertheless, this is all leading up to personal practice and play on public and club courts – as with most sports. So the pupil should be encouraged and helped during school P.E. and games sessions to learn about the need for basic tennis clothing related to climate and warm-up (even if it is not required 'strip' for actual school games periods).

Pre-game warm-up and practice: track suit for cold, inclement weather; wool sweater or sports cardigan for warmer days, to avoid chilled or torn muscles. This protective top-clothing is then normally removed before the actual match, once the muscles are warm and limber. In fact, it is considered bad form to continue wearing the track suit during the match. But at least, the warm clothing is ready to hand to replace as soon as the games are over, and if there is a chance of taking a shower, so much the better. If not, a strip-wash and a brisk rub-down is the next best

Tennis for Schools

thing – and most certainly, we would hope, a change of underwear (a big argument for the sports bag).

It's obvious from all this, that there's more to serious tennis than a casual playground knock-about; but with a lot of young fellas and girls, I suppose it's mostly a matter of 'take your pick'. Maybe this is where the pre-adult conditioning in junior school can be so useful.

To end on a cheerful colour note – admittedly I put in my vote for all-white tennis strip; but rationally there's no reason why a splash of colour shouldn't brighten-up the court. So if the big international players are wearing red, yellow or blue T-shirts as part of their identification, I honestly can't say why our boys and girls shouldn't do the same; but leave off the slogans and badges, we're not promoting a cult.

By the way, have they got that largish, absorbent towel for the post-game cool-down?

4

'Free Play', or Direct Teaching?

Free play or practice without direct teaching and coaching is essential. The players will be doing plenty of it in their own time for fun and leisure, maybe for exercise if they feel inclined, so the younger they get the hang of it the better.

It's also good for encouragement and relaxation during school time: in the actual P.E. lesson, or during break, lunch-hour or after-school recreation. Even so, in these sessions, some unobtrusive observation and check is necessary, if only for safety and the preservation of equipment!

Many teachers see free play as a form of vital 'self-learning' and strongly believe in this self-discovery method of bringing pupils on. Yet direct teaching has to come in somewhere, else how would sound technical knowledge and real improvement of the game be gained?

There the basic grips, stance, strokes and playing postures and positions to be recognised and applied. That is, if they are to be performed with maximum efficiency and minimum errors in the formative stages.

Unlimited 'free' practice alone is unlikely to serve this purpose. Especially as some teachers consider tennis to be one of the more difficult sports to learn. Certainly not so easily picked-up as soccer, for example. 'Definitely needs special teaching and coaching, not just left to the pupil.' So says one of my P.E. colleagues. I'm with her all the way. I must, she's my wife!

Limitations of un-coached practice

'Do-as-you-please' (seemingly), 'find out for yourself' education has its place. Yet you know, it never is as truly do-as-you-please as it may seem to the casual observer. It's always subtly controlled by serious planning. And, with serious tennis, or the introduction of the beginner to it, no one is capable of developing his top potential of performance without skilled, sympathetic advice, instruction and guidance at a personal level. And this despite the protests of the 'free play' fraternity, who claim that teacher interference too early may destroy the essential fun factor and dampen the child's 'voluntary appetite'.

The chief drawback of uncoached practice, is the inability of the average performer to 'feel', interpret and understand, or even direct the functioning of his own motor muscles in every situation. He is performing spontaneously according to his responses, albeit, enjoying himself, Yes, he is playing and learning.

He sees the ball approaching and moves in to hit it. He probably does hit it, most of the time, with or without recognisable style; but does the ball go exactly where he wants it to? Is he capable of developing his own brand of skill and precision to a high enough standard, merely by uncoached practice? Has he enough self-awareness through this undisciplined play-learning.

In any case, has the uncoached performer sufficient knowledge and grasp of skills and tactics to sustain interest and enthusiasm? Or is boredom more likely to result after the first few minutes of unrestricted knock-about, unskilled activity? The teacher obviously has to come up with some practical answers.

Movement distortion and habitual errors

During 'play' time, how does the untutored performer know he is using his total body to its best advantage – unless he has a highly developed self-wareness of himself in action – and 'action feed-back', which he can interpret for self correction and improvement – or even want to?

How is he to know if he is grooving-in a distorted stance, or ugly movement by countless repetitions of a habitual bodily error or malfunction?

Has he any real movement or kinaesthetic sense at this stage that will feed back a mirrored image of himself in action, so that he can observe from within, interpret the bodily fault and issue the necessary directives to his motor muscles to avoid repetition of the distortion?

Such malfunctioning generally develops from a form of spontaneous 'compromise', unknowingly adapting the body to an action crisis by instinctive corrective motion.

With the untrained, non-athletic human, this invariably results

'Free Play', Or Direct Teaching?

in static or dynamic postural distortion and inefficient management of his own body. On the other hand, trained dancers, gymnasts, divers, trampolinists, skaters and pole-vaulters have highly developed bodily control and sense of themselves in action; just as animals have subconsciously with their superior reflexes and functional beauty. Our tennis players need to be trained to develop some of this superior athletic performance and certainly must acquire a firmly-rooted and reliable kinaesthetic sense. Anyway, this is basic with all sports.

This surely is not too idealistic? Although I grant you that many teachers would despair of ever introducing this theme and quality of intimate body awareness to youngsters on the courts with any hope of understanding or success. Hence the popularity of letting them 'find out for themselves'. This is also thought to be easier on the teacher.

Now with the untrained performer, hundreds of these compensatory distortions occur throughout a playing or practice session. Unless the player has a highly observant coach or teacher, interpreting and guiding his movements, how is he to notice and correct his own malfunctioning?

Can an uncoached performer be aware of this instinctive, compensatory mechanism within himself responding to an action crisis? Can he know if this unconscious self-correction is right or wrong?

By chance, he may use his bone levers, joints and motor muscles with a spontaneous anatomical correctness for any one movement in a rally, especially if he has had time to figure it out in advance ('reading the play').

But equally, an action crisis may trigger a panic response or excited reaction, resulting in a momentary domination of his nervous system by the over-riding urge to hit the ball, come what may, regardless of stance, or how he moves in to perform the shot.

This is how movement distortion occur, and how unobserved, uncoached, unchecked repetitions of the fault groove-in a habitual malfunction. Poor style and inefficient playing ability must inevitably result, however initially impressive a 'natural' performer he may appear to be.

THE BIG QUESTION IS, DO YOU ALLOW HIM TO DEVELOP THIS SELF-TAUGHT NATURAL STYLE BEFORE INTRODUCING CORRECTIVE COACHING? ARE YOU AFRAID OF SPOILING HIS FUN BY INTRODUCING

DIRECT TEACHING TOO SOON? OR DO YOU CONDITION YOUR BEGINNER INTO THE 'CLASSIC', STANDARD TENNIS STYLE OF STANCE AND STROKING FROM THE OUTSET, AIMING TO PREVENT MOVEMENT DISTORTION?

Movement reflexes

These are built-in by countless repetitions of a specified reaction to stimuli ('Pavlov's dog'!).

The dilemma facing our player (and coach); is he grooving-in the right or wrong reflexes? (Although I don't suppose our young untutored player worries or even knows about this).

Will repeated practise of directly taught 'classic' (standard) stroke play build in to his nervous system the most efficient, functional responses to play stimuli, (hitting the ball)?

Or alternatively, will he develop this ultimate skill and efficiency simply by unlimited 'free' practice, (the 'self-discovery' method) without the benefit (or hindrance of a dominant coach?)

Natural versus coached player?

We are constantly seeking the answer to the hazy problem that bothers and frustrates many teachers, of practically all subjects. We are probing it through the physical-mental-sensual experience of tennis.

Will a player, starting as a beginner, develop sufficient *'kinetic sense'* of his own body in action, to emerge as a skilled, 'natural' performer, if left alone to practise and discover his own game his own way?

Subsequently, would this natural player with a flair, be able to hold his own in competitive situations of a top club, county, or even national level? Or would he simply be content to get all the pleasure he needs from the game (his form of game) at the local tennis court with his pals. Here he may well enjoy a modest reputation for being quick on the ball, with a repertoire of formidable, natural strokes and a sensitive touch.

This is synonymous with the 'back-street' soccer player, who develops his flair for controlling the ball by endless sessions from an early age with his neighbourhood pals in the streets near his home. Can tennis really be equated with this sort of development? Must the over-riding concession to the fun-factor

'Free Play', Or Direct Teaching?

predominate; or just when can serious teaching and learning be introduced? Oh, this is an intensely individual situation, with probably no hard and fast ruling applicable.

Some teachers (perhaps many) like to believe that 'Teaching to avoid mistakes' is an old-fashioned concept. But does a driving school believe in promoting 'find out for yourself' methods?

Do you allow children to play with hazardous instruments, tools or equipment in the school lab or workshop; or take a motor-scooter or mini on to the street, or a sailing dingy on to the lake, without adequate, professional tuition?

Why should learning of athletic and game skills be treated differently? Aren't they that important? Well, pupils aren't allowed unsupervised practice of athletic field events (shot, discus, javelin) because of the safety factor. But thousands of children do gain their games experience by uncoached, free play, either by deliberate self-discovery procedure, or because of lazy teachers.

Is tennis to come into this category?

'Rather idealistic and gives the impression you are mainly interested in only teaching those children who want to be taught. What about the others?' A fair comment from a P.E. specialist. The answer is, this section on direct teaching is intended for the teacher and coach. Their handling of it will decide what pupils will get. They will also ensure that the fun factor is not destroyed. The gifted teacher has ways and means.

Key words and phrases

Free play
Fun factor
Movement distortion
Habitual errors
Action feed-back
Self-correction
Grooving-in
Movement sense
Kinaesthetic
Observe from within
Spontaneous compromise
Action crisis
Self-development

Functional beauty
Compensatory distortions
Compensatory mechanism
Reading the play
Panic response
Excited reaction
Habitual malfunction
Corrective coaching
Movement reflexes
Self-discovery
Dominant coach
Kinetic sense

5

The Boredom Factor

A P.E. Inspector I know was discussing the tendency that still exists of over-emphasising teaching of technique too early in sports coaching. This practice, he considered, was out-dated and eroded the pupil's interest and enjoyment.

The inflexible adherence to standard technique procedures makes it difficult for the pupil to sustain his initial interest. Because of this he more often than not loses any interest he may have started with and fails to follow-through with improved performance. In fact, the sport is often killed for this pupil by such stereotyped teaching.

Yet technique has to be taught sometime, if the pupil is to gain a reasonably serious grasp of the sport for improved performance, possibly leading to membership of the school team and a little later, the outside club.

So the issue is, not if technique should be taught, but when it shall be introduced and how. Theoretically, as there are many different teaching techniques and presumably most of them well covered at training college, there shouldn't be too much trouble in gaining and sustaining pupils' interest – theoretically, you understand.

Fun and competition

Progressive educators who are loyal to the 'Self-discovery' method and decry the heavy plodding practice of teacher-dominated, standardised technique, constantly remind us that fun and competition are pupils' chief motivation.

A boy (or a girl) wants the satisfaction of 'having a go' with the least delay. He wants to feel and hear the thump of boot or bat on ball; he wants lots of opportunity for kicking and hitting – to be able to work-out (or play-out) his own image. So let him have a go. This provides the fun factor and prevents (or delays) boredom, improves class control – and loses more balls.

Does technique come into it?

Perhaps it all depends upon how keen the teacher is. I suppose it could only be too easy to stand by and watch pupils having a go, without jeopardising their fun by teacher intervention with boring training technique. But direct teaching has to be introduced sometime, somewhere; the main problem is when and how? And does it have to be boring?

Simplifying the issue, it seems that you observe your pupils enjoying themselves freely, with school equipment, then approach the individual with this popular catch-phrase: 'See if you can get better results by hitting the ball this way...' Or even: 'Try holding the racket this way for a change...' So technique is introduced with as least disturbance (or even alienation) as possible. We want these kids to keep on trying, don't we?

Don't we teach to avoid mistakes?

Next thing you know, you're up to the ears in earnest teaching. Or are you? What was that? 'Teaching to avoid mistakes?' Now that's a tricky one. From what I've said, it might be misconstrued that you let them make their mistakes, as a kind of excuse or reason for bringing-in technique – acceptably.

After all, they've got to *want* to learn, haven't they?

Whose responsibility?

I've always promoted the practice of pupils *earning the right* to play sessions in lesson-time by applying themselves diligently to the learning process – showing willing. The traditional system was to get the warm-up and skill-training part of the lesson nicely buttoned-up early-on, go into small group practices, then if the kids had deserved it – end up with a spirited team game, or maybe two or three.

Nowadays, unless you are a particularly gifted and imaginative teacher, the inference is, that if you adopt this warm-up and skill-training lark too soon, you are likely to end up without a class. They've deserted you for more interesting, enjoyable pastimes.

As games and sports 'options' are now presented in the early secondary years, and as much of the P.E. programme is no longer compulsory, the onus for holding on to a class's attention (and attendance) is one more responsibility of the teacher – or an old one brought out into the open.

Hungry for instruction

Just how do you stimulate a class to become hungry for instruction? Educational theory has it that instead of risking boredom and a 'dead' activity on your hands by static teaching of standard technique, you allow the pupils to have a go – which presumably was all they were interested in originally. Then, at the right psychological moment, just before they begin showing signs of self-boredom and declining skill (if they ever started with any), you approach with your artful (and disguised) technique suggestions. Handled right, they are supposed to snap them up – and you have an enlivened class on your hands, hungry for instruction. Mind you, this is a suggestion.

6

Enlarging on Practical Reminders for the Teacher

1. *Teacher or coach? How do you see the difference?* He or she is referred to as teacher rather than coach, because in this context his other role is very much involved in an educational-come-instructional relationship, spanning a time and ability range from complete beginner to member of school team or club.

Considerable know-how and experience of teaching technique, pupil and class discipline and management, planning and promotion of practices and competition, plus progressive, individual coaching, all fall within the duties and responsibilities of the teacher. The universal question is: 'Can I handle it?'

To be truly effective, such a person needs a recognised, professional training background of school teaching by the Department of Education, as well as the specialised qualification of coaching certificates for individual sports, awarded by the governing bodies themselves.

This form of qualified teacher could be said to be truly well-equipped to take on the responsibility of teaching tennis in (or out of) school. This way the teacher should have ample confidence in her or himself, while there should be every reason for the pupil to develop this confidence *in the teacher*.

2. *Develop and maintain a two-way relationship of mutual confidence.* This two-way, teacher-pupil relationship needs to be constantly worked for and maintained. It is a mutual responsibility of continual awareness and endeavour. It is impossible to attach it with greater importance to one or other of the parties involved. Such a relationship once embarked becomes irretrievably involved – or should we say it needs to be for the subsequent health, effectiveness and satisfaction of the participants. It needs to be kept at the head of the priority list.

3. *Variety in teaching and practice – essential:*
   (a) to stimulate interest and enthusiasm.
   (b) to avoid boredom and wandering attention.
   (c) to encourage (persuade?) the pupil to learn.
4. *Plan for maximum pupil participation:*
   (a) to achieve greatest class coverage for fitness and learning.
   (b) to produce most effective and economical use of time, space, equipment.
5. *Necessary to achieve minimum inactivity or idleness by pupils:*
   (a) to avoid wastage of both teacher's and pupils' time and equipment.
   (b) to maintain maximum learning potential.
6. *Aim for a high level of personal example* – in cleanliness, neatness, posture, stance, courtesy, good manners, sportsmanship, fitness and performance. This is a genuine professional way of gaining attention and respect from pupils. Other ways, seemingly popular with some staff (the 'hairy hippie' approach) are doubtful (putting it mildly), at least for mature staff. Anyway, why should they choose to look like pathetic followers of a teenage cult, rather than respected leaders of an adult generation?
7. *Considerate and advantageous positioning of class and teacher.* The teacher should face the sun, if there has to be a choice, to avoid having pupils squint into it. Wind direction needs to be considered too, in connection with the carrying qualities of the teacher's voice.
8. *Careful lesson planning for maximum effective use of equipment, space and personnel.* Teaching is not an activity that can be left to chance or on-the-spot inspiration – well, only now and then. An aura of workmanlike confidence is quickly generated when the teacher has planned and studied in advance what he wants to teach. There is also less stress likely to gum things up in both teacher and class (i.e., the main reason for stress will be removed).
9. *Encourage pupil initiative, co-operation and self-directed discipline.* These three factors in the teaching business are largely what it is all about, irrespective of the subject matter. Tennis provides ideal opportunity and circumstances for fulfilling this self-discipline aspect of education, with excellent potential.
10. *Development of most effective class teaching procedure.* This

Enlarging on Practical Reminders

is aligned with routine and work rhythm. The aim is to conduct the teaching sessions with minimum of misunderstanding and time wastage, at the same time to realise the maximum educational potential of the class period. This can be done by using a teaching technique that attracts and holds the pupils' attention and active interest with the minimum delay. Developing an acceptable work rhythm offers the class a routine with which they are happy to identify. They proffer in return their enthusiastic co-operation. This gets results.

11. *Ways of incorporating individual attention and coaching into the class situation.* Although I have been emphasising the importance of class procedures, much effectiveness is lost unless each individual class member is encouraged to feel personally noticed, recognised and important in his or her own right. A teaching method has to be practised that permits the *individual development* of each pupil within the framework of the class and permits him or her to be recognised and rewarded. This is basic teaching philosophy.

12. *A progress record by 'log book' or card system recommended.* This ties in closely with number 11 above. The individual's progress needs to be regularly noted, recorded and assessed. The pupil concerned needs to be informed and encouraged to compete at two levels:

(1) to improve on his own progress and development.
(2) to feel the urge to improve on the progress of his class colleagues.

The competitive impulse is a natural and healthy human instinct and provides incentive for personal progress combined with *fun, enjoyment* and *fulfilment*.

The maintenance of these three basic factors in the educational/instructional context ensures the undiminished attention and unflagging interest of the pupil, combined with his desire to improve. (Oh, if this was all there was to it!)

Part Two

Grips, Footwork, Stance and Strokes

* FIRM, FAMILIAR GRIPS *weld the racket handle to the player's hand as a natural-seeming extension of the striking arm.*

* GOOD FOOTWORK *carries the power-unit of the player about the court with maximum speed, grace and skilful timing and the minimum stress and fatigue.*

* WELL-DEVELOPED STANCE *places and holds the player's body and limbs in the most advantageous positions from which to make the strongest, most effective and attractive strokes.*

* SKILFUL, CONFIDENT STROKES *place the racket-head in its most effective striking relationship with the ball, to produce a devastating missle of varying, controlled velocity, predetermined flight and accuracy.*

SPECIAL NOTE: in this section, the special instructional plates are designed to be used by the teacher with individual pupils, by classes, or coaching groups, and by noticeboard promotion.

7

Difference in Basic Learning Situations

1. STROKE PRODUCTION: learning how to perform an individual stroke from the beginning, leading up to confidence and familiarity in use.
2. STROKE USE: how you actually use a particular stroke in a practice or games situation to achieve a desired effect.

This section on GRIPS, FOOTWORK, STANCE AND STROKES is confined to selected, simplified descriptions of the purely technical side of *stroke production*.

These four factors are married and indispensable to one another, because tennis is essentially a *game of movement* and constantly changing, dynamic postures. Even in the seemingly stationary 'Ready Position' the performer is never still, but using the time to make little checks on his grip, feel and balance of the racket, and his body generally, particularly the flexibility and power of his legs, ankles and feet.

The following factors in sequence indicate standard stroke production:

POISE – WATCH – MOVE – PLACE – CONTROL – TIMING – STROKE – RECOVER

Concentration and balance are essential throughout.

Once a basic understanding of how the various grips, footwork and strokes are married, technically-speaking, then the very next task for teacher and pupil is how those strokes are applied to suit certain situations. This is then *stroke use*.

8

The Strokes: swing — throw — punch push — block — touch

The main arsenal

FOREHAND (flat-looped swing)	flat/topspin/slice
BACKHAND (straight swing)	lifted/sliced/topspin/backspin
RETURN OF SERVICE (shorter swing)	either of above
SERVICE (throw)	flat/direct 'cannon-ball'/spin/slice/angled
SMASH (throw)	direct/angled/projectile velocity
VOLLEY (punch or block)	wide/low/high/tight
LOB (short lifted swing)	rolled/topspin/offensive/defensive
HALF-VOLLEY (block and push) (touch shot)	long contact and follow-through/hit in no-man's land

Special strokes for improving players

LOB VOLLEY (touch shot)	punch over opponent's head with whole arm, stiff wrist/*very firm*
DROP VOLLEY (touch shot)	used on slow balls/sharp underspin/no follow-through
STOP VOLLEY (touch shot)	to take the pace off fast balls
SLICE (touch shot)	short swing/underspin/sidespin/long contact

The Strokes

CUT, CHOP, CHIP (touch shots) — convenience, opportunity shots/short, sharp underspin/heavily cut is a 'chop' cut and move in is 'chip-approach'

RE-ACTION STROKE (reflex) — not a consciously learnt action, but entirely dependent upon natural flair, quick-trigger thinking and fast reflexes. Essentially a clean-up defensive stroke – played 'off the cuff', although it can often turn a defensive situation into an unpredicted attack.

NOTE: although this is a run-down of standard and advanced strokes that a trained player could be expected to draw upon – eventually, it is not expected that this near complete arsenal would be handled by regular P.E. classes, but would need supporting and developing by extra-curricular coaching and membership of an out-of-school club.

9

Stroke Play: Standard Factors

The impulse to strike is not contained or restricted within the striking arm, or even on that side of the body alone. It is a total body impulse that surges and flows through every nerve and muscle fibre.

* Watch the ball keenly, be aware of your footwork.
* Think ahead of the stroke, move into the shot and be on top of the play.
* Be aware of foot placement and body positioning.
* The foot leads the movement into the shot.
* The body positions itself behind and around the leading foot.
* The free arm guides and balances.
* The racket arm prepares for the stroke, moves into the ball, feels for it, makes long contact through the strings, sweeps it forward and follows-through along the line of the shot.
* Aim to take the ball just ahead of or in front of the body – as an *attacking* stroke. Don't wait to be overtaken by the ball. Decide if it is to be an attacking strike or defensively, a *clean-up stroke*.
* Watch the ball right on to your racket strings and aim for a long contact between them (as against a hardboard bounce).
* Go through the strokes in your mind whenever you are temporarily inactive; wherever you are: waiting for a bus, in the lunch queue, when out walking in the countryside (but not cycling or motoring); during jogging, training, sunbathing. . . .

Fundamental principles:
The 'classic style' still operates, but deviations from this are

Stroke Play: Standard Factors

quite in order to suit individual characteristics and flair. Certain *basic fundamentals* however, are unwavering in their importance:
(1) Balance, concentration and steadiness of mind
(2) Footwork
(3) Feel and control of racket
(4) Swing: (backswing, forward stroke, strike, follow-through)
(5) Watching the ball and anticipating play

A well-considered, confident blend of these gives that smooth fluency which creates a deceptive impression of simplicity and ease.

Balance: this ensures good control. When good balance is maintained, the racket can be used in the manner desired. In *over-balance*, arms are automatically used to recover and control of the racket is reduced. Loss of balance is often caused by undue use of weight to increase stroke power.

TIMING IS MORE IMPORTANT THAN STRENGTH

Basic technique with individual style

It is well to get across to pupils as early as you think fit, that although they are having to learn strokes through the careful practice and repetition of basic techniques, this isn't going to restrict their personal progress. They will be developing their own style and flair – but still built up on standard stroke production, which is the bedrock of sound, confident and accurate tennis.

Starting with standard or basic techniques, they will develop and adapt these as they progress to suit the feel of their bodies and responses in action. They will be rewarded with an individual way of playing tennis that works for them.

10

Basic Essential Grips

Starting with basics and getting acquainted with the racket by shaking hands with it. This will introduce beginners to the three most comfortable and practical grips they need to start with: FOREHAND, BACKHAND, SERVICE and SMASH.

When a comfortable and familiar grip has been moulded to the hand, it becomes an instinctive part of the player to pick up and transmit all the attacking or defensive impulses of the nervous system and motor muscles through the racket, which is used either as a weapon of precision, or a medium of art, according to the circumstances and the mood.

Forehand Grip

Also known as the 'Eastern Grip' and the 'Shake-hands' grip. To simplify instruction, you can speak only of the latter. It carries a clear image.

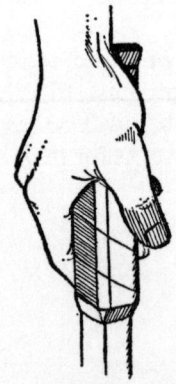

Fig. 15. 'Shake-hands' grip

Basic Essential Grips

CHECK-LIST ON THE FOREHAND GRIP

* Support racket at its throat by fingers of non-playing hand, its face on edge vertically, and its butt towards the body. Place palm of playing hand flat against the strings and draw it back towards handle, then grasp the leather grip when it is snugly alongside the palm.

* Separate the first finger slightly for extra control and improved feel. This finger should make a 'v' with the thumb on the top edge of the handle.

* Palm of hand is behind or at the back of the handle, similar to the position you would adopt to hit the ball with the flat hand.

* Leather butt is to be tucked snugly into or against the heel of the hand.

* Spread the remaining fingers a little for improved strength and comfort. Avoid forming a tight fist around the grip.

* Wriggle the grip a bit in your palm until it feels just right and comfortable – and what is most important, a natural and powerful extension of your arm.

* Now check position of racket head:
  (1) it should be cocked-up slightly from the hand, just above the horizontal.
  (2) The racket face should be inclined at an angle according to the direction of aim – slightly upwards for low balls, downwards for balls higher than net height. This will give greater control and direction to the flight of the ball.

These notes give the position and control of the racket during the action of striking the ball with the forehand drive. There can be variations, but we shall not elaborate at this stage of learning. The one overall factor to keep in mind is that the grip you adopt should feel right, comfortable and powerful for you. It becomes your personal way of holding the racket, your individual way of welding the racket handle to your hand.

Backhand Grip

The forehand grip has to be changed to the backhand during the fast action of play, so both grips must be thoroughly learnt and constantly practised, until adopting one or the other becomes instinctive within a second's notice. After a while, there should be no more fumbling, but a direct, clean, instant grasp.

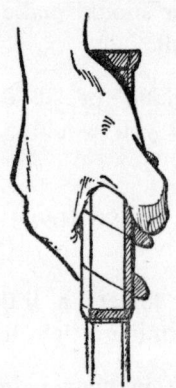

Fig. 16. Backhand grip

CHECK-LIST ON BACKHAND GRIP

* Support racket by its throat: loosen the forehand grip, turn and regrasp nearly a quarter-turn anti-clockwise to adopt the new backhand grip. The strings are still vertical to the ground.

* Palm is now located on top of the handle (instead of behind it), with the base of the *thumb* now placed at the back of the grip and the thumb diagonally across it. This can exert a bracing and steadying effect on the racket face at the instant of impact with the ball.

* Separate the first finger again (along the front face of the grip this time). The 'V' it makes with the thumb should now be directly over the left bevel of the grip.

* Avoid overdoing the bracing effect of the thumb. In other words, don't just place it along the back of the handle like

Basic Essential Grips

a splint. The backhand grip must still permit some flexibility and adaptability, although the wrist joint must have strength and firmness at impact when required.

* Butt of racket should be tucked up firmly against the fleshy heel of the striking hand.

* The non-playing hand occupies a key role by controlling the change-over. The supporting fingers at the racket's throat perform the twisting action as the racket is swung back, positioning the grip in the striking hand ready for the swing forward and backhand drive. This smooth, fast change of grip becomes instinctive and secure with plenty of practice.

* Position of racket head during moment of strike and impact should be cocked slightly above horizontal as with the forehand grip and drive.

Even if a beginner's first experience of the backhand may seem awkward, his confidence can be greatly increased by bearing in mind that the backhand striking action is a strongly natural one with man. There is the familiar action of tossing rings, and dealing cards, for example – and even the sharp aggressive jab backwards with the elbow.

Service and Smash Grip

Initially, the same 'Shake-hands' grip can be effectively and comfortably used for both these strokes. Later, as skill and confidence increases noticeably, variations of this grip can be learnt and built-in to the pupil's skill bank. This would be a highly individual change-over for advanced players, with the pupil's progress being the yardstick for the coach to observe and interpret. Meanwhile, stick to the basic 'Shake-hands' grip. It is the mechanics and the feel of the basic serving action that is important at the beginning. Subtle reactions of 'whip', 'kick' and spin can be gained later by minor grip adjustment, principally to the 'Chopper' grip. With regular practice this can become second nature, and a deadly attacking weapon in a player's armoury.

Tennis for Schools

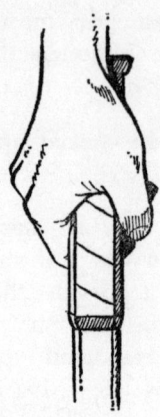

Fig. 17. Service grip – 'Chopper'

CHECK-LIST ON THE SERVICE AND SMASH GRIP

* Beginners are advised to start with the original forehand grip – the *Shake-hands* grip. This will let the learner become familiar with the technique and feel of the serve, without adding complications of grip variation.

* When the pupil is beginning to overflow with confidence and the old all-purpose Shake-hands grip is clearly no longer good enough, then it is time to introduce the more specialised *Chopper* grip.

* But with beginners, aim for a fair mastery of the forehand grip for service first. At the same time, never hide from them that they will shortly be learning the recognised *Chopper* grip, it is the most effective grip for serving and reaching up to smash high balls, permitting more flexibility of the wrist.

* It is called the 'Chopper' grip because of its similarity to the grip used with a hand-axe or a hammer, with more of the palm on the top side (or bevel) of the handle.

* Wrap the thumb around the handle and separate the forefinger slightly for extra support.

* This grip encourages a good wristy movement to develop plenty of snap into the throwing action of serving.

Basic Essential Grips

* Check this grip by bouncing a ball with the edge of the racket. This little test should demonstrate the effectiveness of the grip.
* Use the non-playing fingers to steady the racket by its throat while the small variations of grip change-over are being made.
* The two main advantages of the chopper grip are: it permits more wrist flexibility and sharper angling of the racket face to the ball – resulting in a more disconcerting spin reaction from the ball when it strikes the opposite court.
* Use this grip for both the service and the smash strokes. It is proven best.

NOTE A: Notes on building these grips into class practice are given at the beginning of Part Three, a little further on.

NOTE B: Remember that, while initially the grip for both service and smash is identical – for convenience, the player should not assume that these strokes are permanently identical. The subtle differences will become apparent to the more practiced player – if not, they should be drawn to his attention.

Pupil Practice

1. Class facing teacher in loose group, with rackets.
2. Teacher demonstrates what 'shaking hands with the racket' means. Shows position of striking hand on and around the grip.
3. Class group opens out, start with racket on ground.
4. Practise picking up racket with non-playing hand, fitting the grip into the palm of the striking hand. Teacher explaining. Repeat many times to achieve familiarity.
5. Teacher moves freely among pupils checking and correcting.
6. *When all grips are learnt,* practise changing from one to another on *teacher signal* to improve readiness and familiarity and sharpen response and reflexes.

Time: 4 minutes plus.

11

The 'Predator' Stance, or 'Ready' Position

These three basic action factors of *footwork, stance* and *strokes* are contained in readiness and calm within the player. They are the result of conscientious learning, practice and conditioning. They combine and blend with harmony into the 'Ready' position, from which the player fires himself into attack or defence – triggered by responses and signals in the opposite court.

The alert, aggressive player is undoubtedly a predator, held on a fine knife-edge of control until responding to the signal to attack – and destroy.

The 'Predator' stance is a state of *relaxed alertness:* a seemingly contradictory psycho-physical condition, which nevertheless prepares and holds the body ready for split-second action. One notes it with the hunting animal.

This is similar in effect to the superbly tuned engine of a top-quality car, held with disengaged gears at controlled idling speed, to engage in a second and surge forward with rapidly increasing power.

The tennis athlete poised in the 'Predator' stance is about to demonstrate his intention and ability to spring to any point of the compass from this position of readiness, with the reflexes and responses of a big cat – instantaneously. He feels he has with superb confidence a command of any area of court from this trigger spot.

The 'Image'

This is the image the tennis player should have of himself. Apart from the everyday motivation of momentary fun and personal pleasure, this self-image of relaxed alertness can generate an unsurpassed intimate pleasure that surges through every body nerve and fibre.

This alone is sufficient to provide the incentive to learn, train and improve at deeper, more intensive levels of concentration and perseverance.

All this is encompassed and manifest by the aware tennis athlete, gathering together and holding the power-unit of his body in this tell-tale posture of the 'Predator' stance. This is the performer instinctively applying biodynamics.

Balanced Resting State

This is the ability to achieve an *easeful* state of *expanded* muscular relaxation in the conscious body. Muscular control of this order is only possible if we are able to start from an easeful, well-balanced state of rest, and know how to return to this relaxed condition when we call 'Stop' to our body's motor-muscle activity and allow these muscles to *lengthen*. Success is ours when we are able to maintain this restful state with *conscious awareness*. Our aim: between bouts of dynamic action, to come back to and maintain – A BALANCED RESTING USE OF OUR BODIES which will LEAST INTERFERE WITH OUR FUNCTIONING.

The 'Predator' stance or 'Ready' position gives us the opportunity to return to this BALANCED RESTING STATE between action, while still aware of and reacting to our relationship with our environment – the tennis court and players. It permits us to collect ourselves, check over and form a clear intention of what to do next. In other words, we are in charge of ourselves – and the situation. This is the vital *kinaesthetic* sense we learn about in a study of biodynamics.

CHECK-LIST OF KEY POINTS

* From the foundation of the feet: comfortably spaced and parallel to provide poise and power. Although the body-weight is held forward over the balls of the feet, the heels are still in contact with the ground to minimise fatigue from over-tense leg muscles.

Tennis for Schools

PREDATOR STANCE

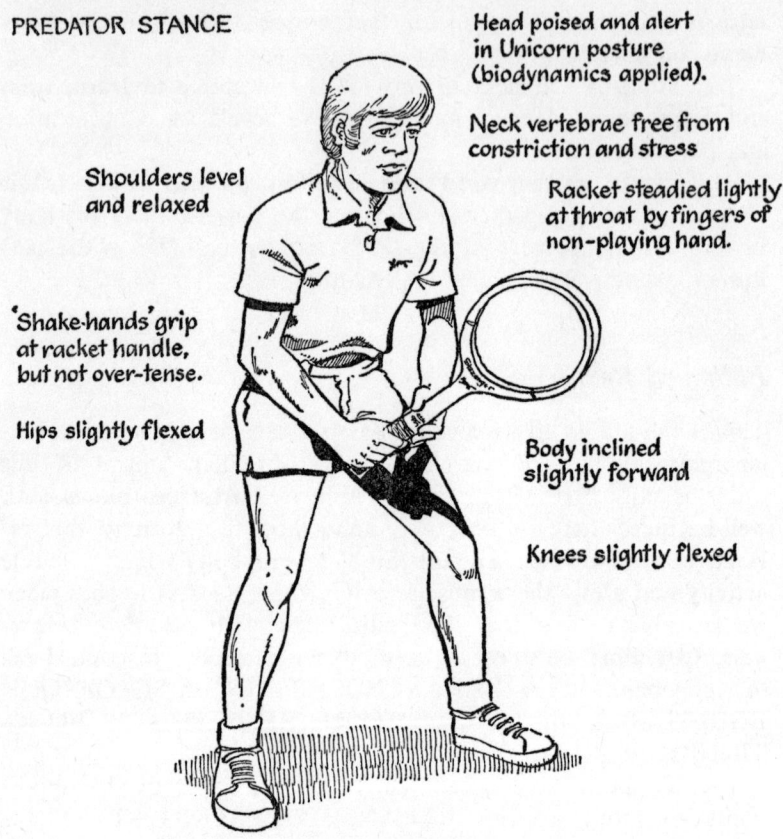

Fig. 18. The 'Predator' stance for receiving

NOTE: position is never completely stationary, but one of constant, imperceptible checking of grip, feel, balance, stance, flexibility and waiting power of the legs, ankles and feet.

A balanced resting state of heightened awareness.

The 'Predator' Stance, or 'Ready' Position

* Knees are slightly flexed, to create and maintain a basic muscular tone within the powerful springs of the thighs.
* Hips are slightly flexed and the trunk inclined forward at a comfortable angle to give the feeling and capability of poise and relaxed power.
* The racket is held by the 'Shake-hands' grip in front of the chest, but not over-tense – which would simply dissipate precious energy.
* The fingers of the non-playing hand lightly steady the racket at its throat, with its head held higher than its butt.
* The shoulders are level and more or less relaxed to avoid unnecessary tension.
* The neck vertebrae are free from constriction and stress, a condition achieved by the correctly-poised head. (Conscious biodynamics are applied to this head-neck region)
* The head is poised in correct alignment with the cervical spine (the neck), in what is known as the 'Unicorn' posture, to prevent constriction, stress and tension in the vertebrae and muscles of that region.
* It helps the performer to visualise this posture and subsequent movement as if being suspended and led by the highest point of the hairline – the brow: 'leading with the brow'.

The natural instinctive stance

Once this position of readiness has been learnt and adopted, it becomes a vital body state at the beginning and the end of any subsequent movement about the court. The player springs into action from this stance, performs his attacking or defensive play, then recovers and returns to his 'Predator' stance from his chosen command postion on the court.

This sequence of adopted stance, subsequent stroke play, recovery and return to the stance, becomes an instinctive, protective response. It is in fact, a conditioned reflex, as effective as the one performed with Pavlov's dog, but encompassing a far wider range of action and reaction.

Tennis for Schools

Pupil Practice

1. Have them 'run the rule' over themselves from the ground upwards, guided by these 'points to check'. Teacher calls out the points in sequence, including necessary explanations.
2. **'Reaction 'Stop and adopt':**
   (a) class moving and milling freely; upon teacher's signal, they jump-turn to face and freeze in the 'Predator' stance.
   (b) class in pairs; free practice at throwing and catching – left- and right-handed. Upon teacher's signal, they catch, face each other and freeze in the stance. Then they check and correct each other's stance as teacher calls out explanatory points.

   Time: 3 minutes, plus.

12

Groundstrokes: Forehand and Backhand Drives

Add knowledge and ability of these two fundamental strokes to the initial 'Ready' position and stimulating practice, even competitive play can be enjoyed. These are the two bedrock, foundation strokes of tennis.

Forehand drive (flat-looped swing)

Grip: Shake-hands grip

Start: Ready position

STROKE PRODUCTION:

(1) Back-swing, pivot and place
(2) Weight transfer, anchor and forward stroke
(3) Watch and strike
(4) Watch and follow-through

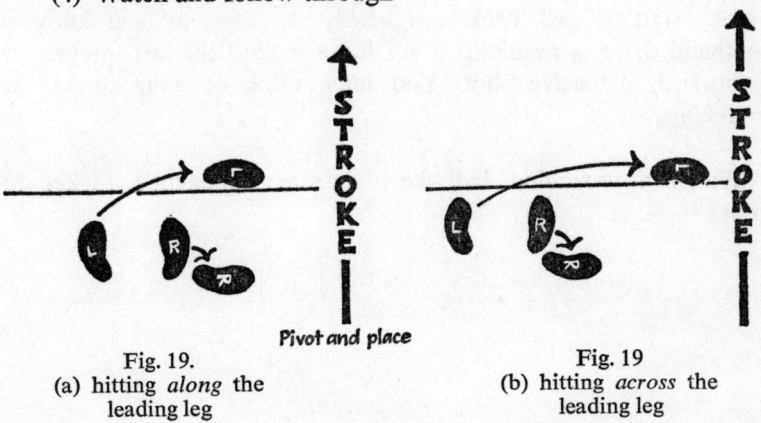

Fig. 19.
(a) hitting *along* the leading leg

Fig. 19
(b) hitting *across* the leading leg

Tennis for Schools

FOREHAND DRIVE

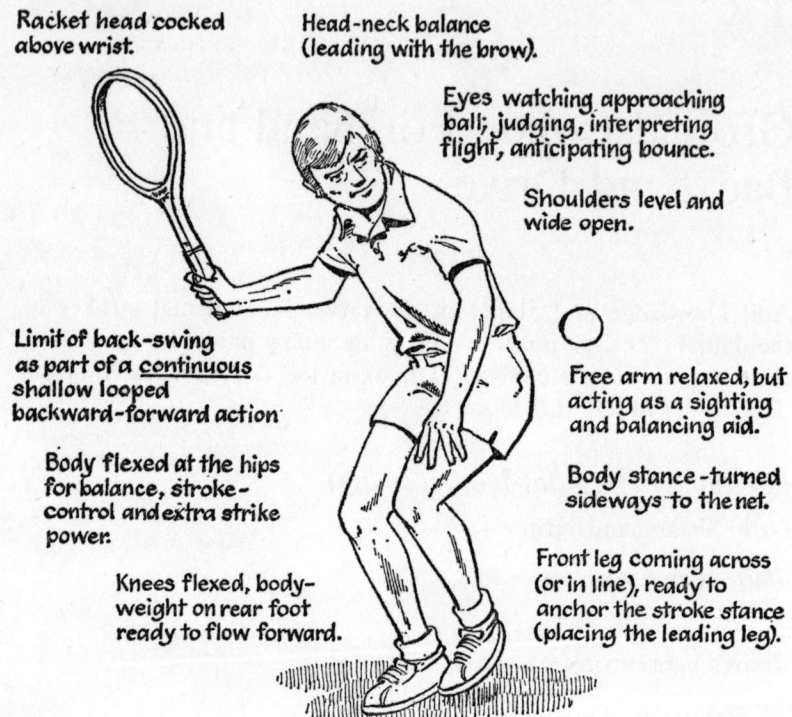

Fig. 20. (1) Back-swing, pivot and place

NOTE: start looped back-swing early, as soon as you know a forehand drive is required; don't leave it until the last minute for a hurried, defensive shot. You must think of your strokes as *attacking*.

Watch approaching ball keenly from opponent's racket to yours.

Groundstrokes: Forehand and Backhand Drives

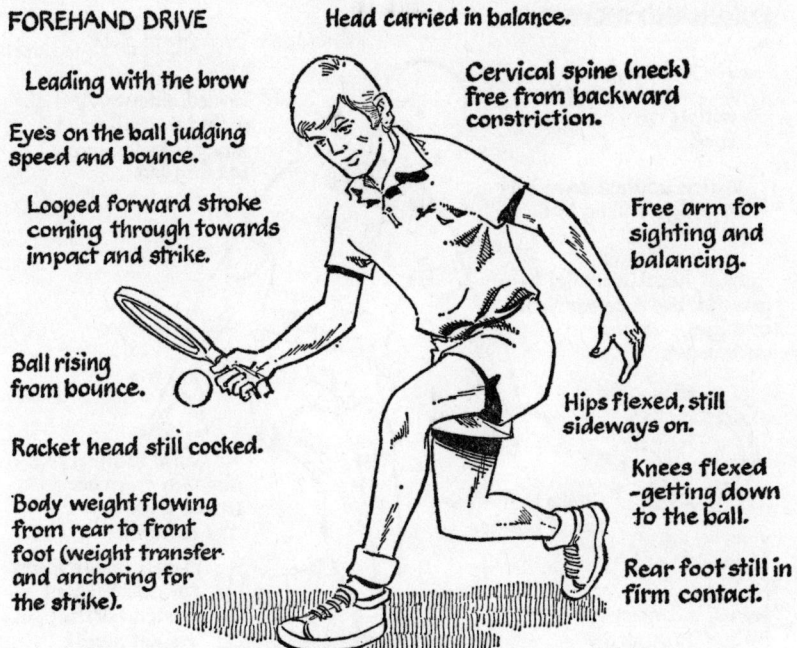

FOREHAND DRIVE

Head carried in balance.

Leading with the brow

Eyes on the ball judging speed and bounce.

Looped forward stroke coming through towards impact and strike.

Cervical spine (neck) free from backward constriction.

Free arm for sighting and balancing.

Ball rising from bounce.

Racket head still cocked.

Body weight flowing from rear to front foot (weight transfer and anchoring for the strike).

Hips flexed, still sideways on.

Knees flexed —getting down to the ball.

Rear foot still in firm contact.

Fig. 21. (2) Weight transfer, anchor and forward stroke

NOTE: foot placement for *every* shot is essential. Aim for placement and positioning to strike *falling* ball (just after the top of bounce), for standard, rallying play. Strike rising ball as an advancing, attacking stroke, when more experienced.

Tennis for Schools

FOREHAND DRIVE

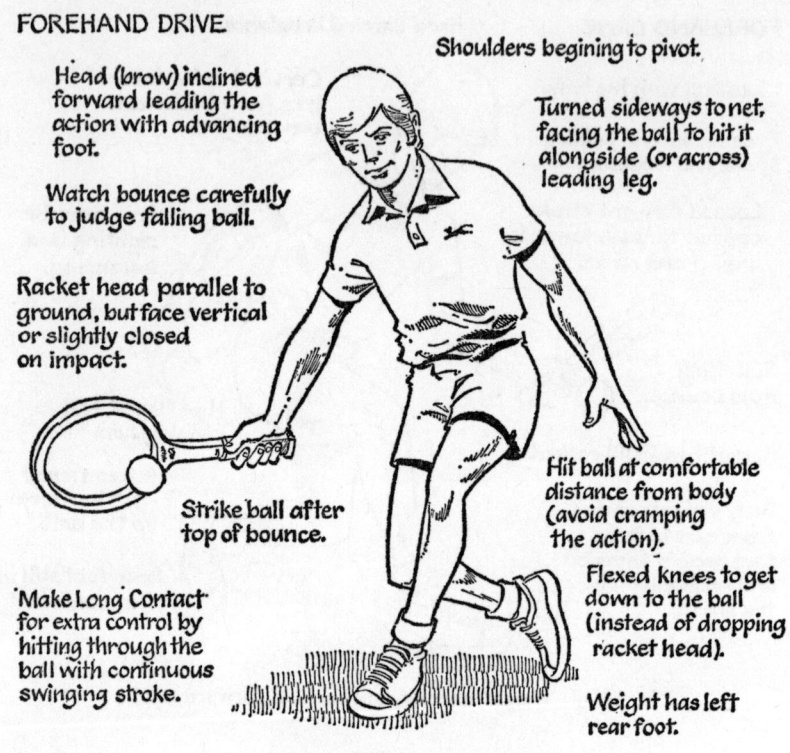

Fig. 22. (3) Watch and strike

NOTE: For low balls, flex knees, get down and apply lift into the stroke; higher balls may require a turning or rolling over of the racket head to bring the ball down with extra control over the net.

'Long contact' means getting the feel of the ball actually on the racket strings and *staying there* for a split second before rebounding – 'gathering' or 'netting' the ball, as against an uncontrolled bounce off a hard surface. This is to gain more ball control and accuracy.

Groundstrokes: Forehand and Backhand Drives

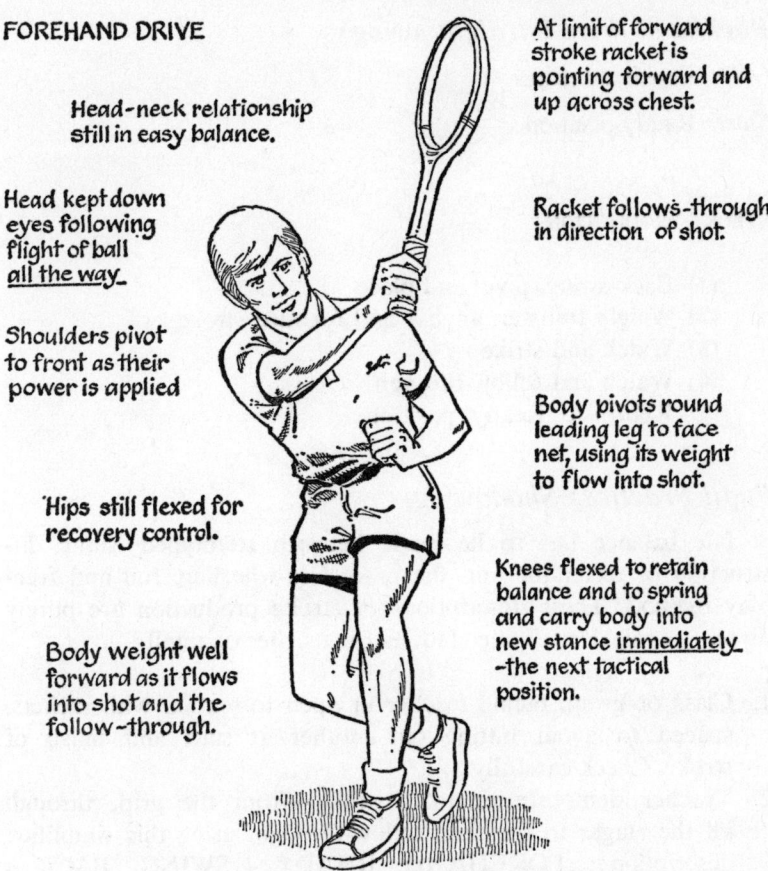

FOREHAND DRIVE

Head-neck relationship still in easy balance.

Head kept down eyes following flight of ball <u>all the way</u>

Shoulders pivot to front as their power is applied

Hips still flexed for recovery control.

Body weight well forward as it flows into shot and the follow-through.

At limit of forward stroke racket is pointing forward and up across chest.

Racket follows-through in direction of shot.

Body pivots round leading leg to face net, using its weight to flow into shot.

Knees flexed to retain balance and to spring and carry body into new stance <u>immediately</u> – the next tactical position.

Fig. 23. (4) Watch and follow-through

NOTE: at no time are the body and limbs straight or without flexion. Power comes from limbs and muscles that are slightly flexed and gathering to spring.

At completion of natural, easy follow-through (following the ball), there is no standing still to admire or bemoan that shot. Anticipation of opponent's return must be immediate, and the move to the next tactical position started with no pause.

Do not jerk head up after strike, but maintain head-neck-shoulder relationship ('Long neck').

Tennis for Schools

Backhand drive (*straight swing*)

Grip: Backhand grip

Start: Ready position

STROKE PRODUCTION:

(1) Back-swing, pivot and place
(2) Weight transfer, anchor and forward stroke
(3) Watch and strike
(4) Watch and follow-through
 Return to 'Ready' position

Pupil Practice: Shadowing

A fair balance has to be made between sterotyped 'static' instruction of technique and the more free-wheeling, fun and free-play method. These descriptions of stroke production are purely direct, technical recommendations for teacher or pupil.

1. Class or group facing teacher in open formation with rackets, spaced to avoid hitting one-another at start and finish of stroke. Check carefully.
2. Teacher demonstrates total stroke – from the grip, through all the stages to the final follow-through, using this simplified description: FOREHAND READY – SWING BACK – SWING FORWARD – FOLLOW-THROUGH.

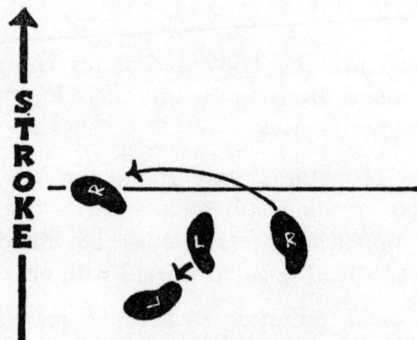

Fig. 24. Pivot and place

Groundstrokes: Forehand and Backhand Drives

3. Class copies his movement, watching him as if watching approaching ball, so they get the general feel of the total stroke, while he calls out the four-part description. Repeat.

Forehand ready. 'Ready' position facing front (net); racket about waist high pointing forward; body weight over balls of feet, knees bent and springy; mind alert.
Swing back. Pivot sideways to net, weight on rear foot; place front foot towards net and tram-lines; swing racket back in a flat loop about waist high until it is in line with shoulders, arm nearly straight, racket head cocked above wrist; leading shoulder aiming in direction of shot. Shoulders open.
Swing forward. Transfer weight to front foot; swing racket into forward stroke with arm almost full stretch; rotate that shoulder and side towards line of stroke; strike ball about waist high (as it begins to fall) and opposite midrif or a little nearer to net. Keep swing continuous and hit through ball with feeling of lift.
Follow-through. Keep racket going through along flight of ball; but let racket head rise gradually after impact to finish-up on opposite side of body, shoulders turned to the front, weight anchored on leading leg to avoid overbalancing. Watch intended flight of ball.

NOTE: bend the knees to low balls, getting more lift into the shot; for higher balls, try to strike with racket face slightly shut to get on top of the ball (turning the racket over).

Backhand ready. Position as for forehand.
Swing back. Pivot sideways to net, weight on rear foot; swing racket across chest towards rear shoulder, taking playing hand well back with bent elbow; turn upper body to show back of striking shoulder towards net, looking back over that shoulder at opponent; racket still supported and guided at throat by non-playing hand, racket head cocked above wrist; place leading foot across towards tram-lines and net; knees bent and springy.
Swing forward. Join backswing to forward stroke with shallow loop, pivoting leading shoulder and hip, round towards front, weight flowing on to forward foot; racket head comes through below point of impact; strike ball opposite leading foot or leading

shoulder at a comfortable arm's length; brush-up back of ball at impact with a feeling of lift.
Follow-through. Racket follows flight of ball, forward and up above net, with striking arm and racket forming unbroken line; pivot the playing shoulder into and with the shot facing the front with open chest; weight mainly on forward foot.

NOTE: whether or not to use a looped or a straight swing for the backhand is a matter of choice; they both have advantages. In any case, try to make the swing smooth and continuous.

This practice is shadowing the strokes without use of ball. It can give pupils an initial impression of basic forehand-backhand movement. But bring in ball practice as soon as possible for more realism, interest and enjoyment. Part Three deals with this.

More on shadowing

Apart from having a whole class do it together, shadowing is also a very personal form of practice. It can be done with or without a racket, preferably with. The idea is to perform strokes *in the mind* and groove them into the nervous system as a form of pre-conditioning for the motor muscles. Do it in the mind at every opportunity when you have minutes to spare (not to the embarrassment of others). Imprint the impression of performing the basic strokes so that the racket becomes a natural extension of your arm, whether it's in your hand or not.

* *Shadow stroking* – grooving the stroke through the mind.
* *Feeling* the stroke through the body.
* *Building-up* a mental stroke bank.
* *Standing outside* yourself to gain a 'photographic' impression of your stance and strokes.
* *Total body involvement* for every stroke is essential, with or without racket.
* *Room practice* in bad weather, or at any spontaneous opportunity.

BACKHAND DRIVE

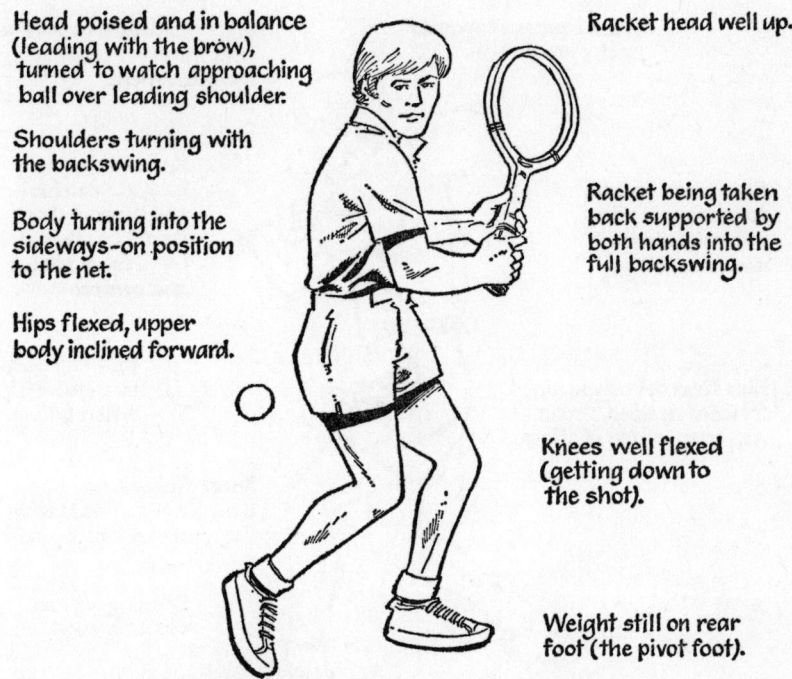

Head poised and in balance (leading with the brow), turned to watch approaching ball over leading shoulder.

Shoulders turning with the backswing.

Body turning into the sideways-on position to the net.

Hips flexed, upper body inclined forward.

Racket head well up.

Racket being taken back supported by both hands into the full backswing.

Knees well flexed (getting down to the shot).

Weight still on rear foot (the pivot foot).

Leading foot coming across ready to place and anchor in the backhand stance.

Fig. 25 (1) Back-swing, pivot and place

NOTE: change the grip from 'Shake-hands' to 'Backhand' from the 'Ready' position as the backswing is started.

Get the racket going across the chest and the shoulders beginning to turn as the feet move in to take their stance; but don't anchor the leading leg too soon.

Tennis for Schools

BACKHAND DRIVE

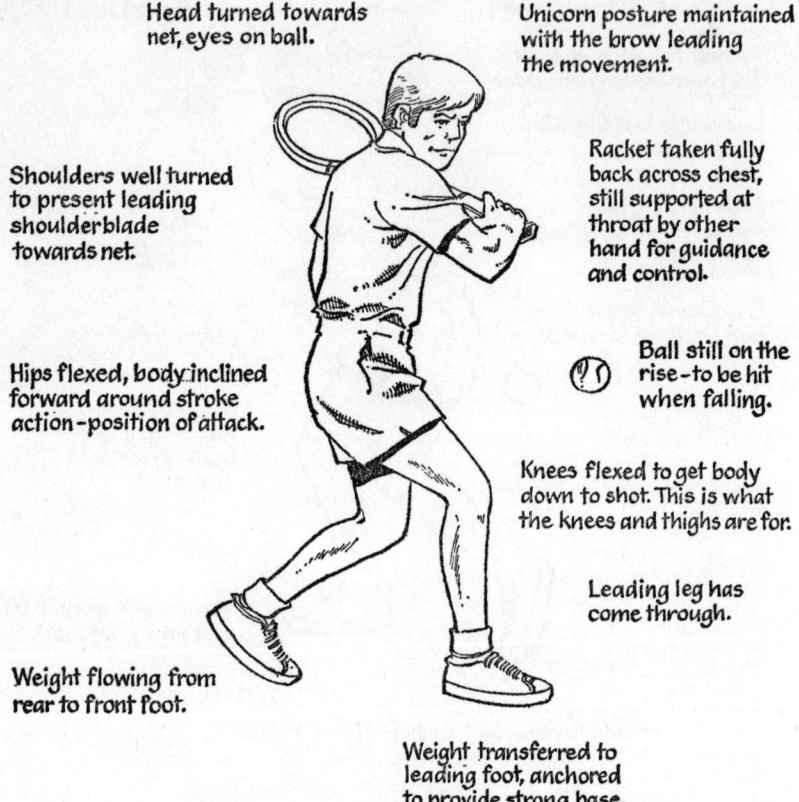

Fig. 26. (2) Weight transfer, anchor and forward stroke

NOTE: always be prepared to go after and get down to low balls by bending the knees, using the thighs as powerful springs. Never give way to laziness or lethargy.

Don't wait for ball to come to you, anticipate its flight, go after it and get into a strong attacking position. Feel you are well on top of your backhand stroke.

Groundstrokes: Forehand and Backhand Drives

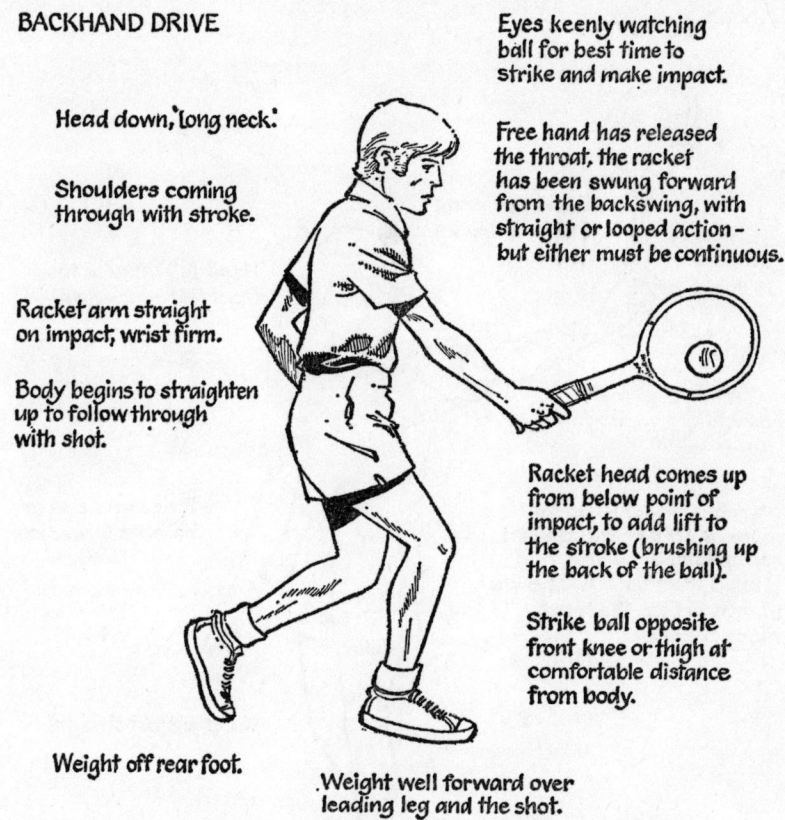

BACKHAND DRIVE

Eyes keenly watching ball for best time to strike and make impact.

Head down, 'long neck'.

Free hand has released the throat, the racket has been swung forward from the backswing, with straight or looped action — but either must be continuous.

Shoulders coming through with stroke.

Racket arm straight on impact, wrist firm.

Body begins to straighten up to follow through with shot.

Racket head comes up from below point of impact, to add lift to the stroke (brushing up the back of the ball).

Strike ball opposite front knee or thigh at comfortable distance from body.

Weight off rear foot.

Weight well forward over leading leg and the shot.

Fig. 27. (3) Watch and strike

NOTE: actual impact with ball may be in line with front knee (getting down to it), or higher according to the type of shot from opponent. It is generally struck more forward than with forehand drive.

Whether or not to use a looped swing is debatable. Some experts prefer the loop for fluency and to disguise their intended shot. Other like the straight swing for improved timing.

Tennis for Schools

BACKHAND DRIVE

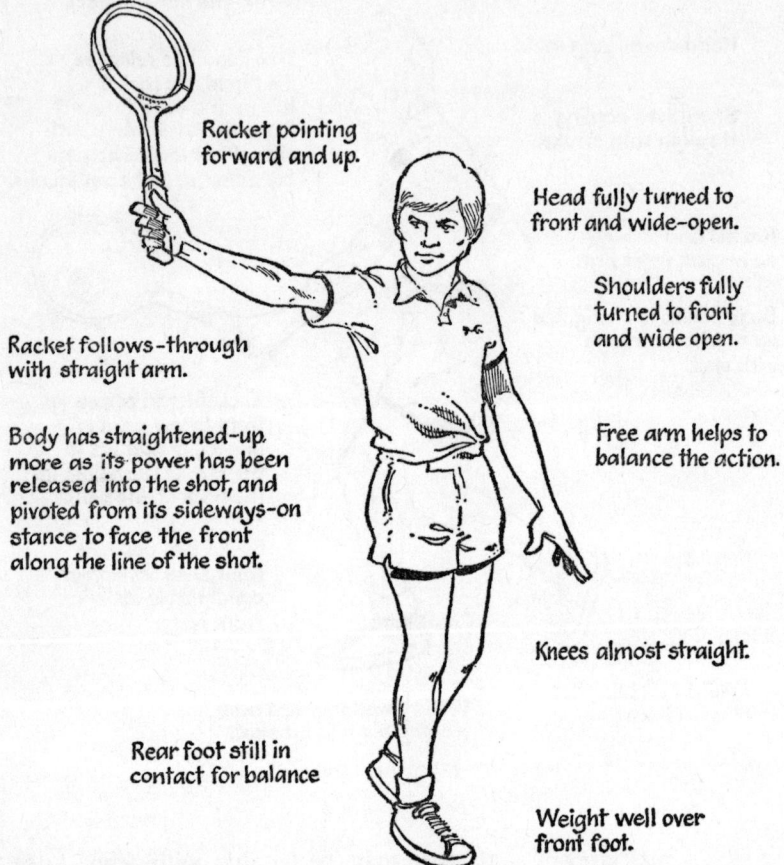

Fig. 28. (4) Watch and follow-through

NOTE: as the strike is made, extra power is gained by pivoting from the sideways-on position to the frontal one. Have the feeling of driving the ball away from you.

The non-racket arm is used more in the backhand stroke, supporting, guiding the backswing and ensuring that the shoulders are kept clear.

13

Service and Smash

Such exciting, satisfying strokes to perform, they must be introduced as early as possible; but I would advise only after the pupil is becoming familiar with using the racket for the two major groundstrokes and getting great satisfaction out of them. Then, on to these two magnificent power-shots.

Every tennis player has an image of himself performing the non-returnable 'ace', or uncoiling powerfully to make the killing smash, like an attacking tiger. So it is logical that they should be brought in right after the groundstrokes. Fortunately, the service doesn't have to be difficult: you place the ball up and then hit it! The smash is a 'sitting duck'!

Beginners' Service (push, pat and throw: 'Shoulder serve')

Grip: 'Shake-hands'

Start: Service position (open stance)

STROKE PRODUCTION

(1) Throwing the ball
(2) Place the ball and let it fall
(3) Ball and racket up together
(4) Push or pat the ball

Never lose sight of the ball!

Tennis for Schools

(1) *Throwing the ball beginners' service*

It is vital to get the proper *over-arm* throwing action built-in to the serve right from the start. This is especially important for girls, who are all too often weak on throwing generally. So over-arm throwing practice for the racket arm is the lead-in for a strong serve to come. But it doesn't have to be prolonged; just enough to get the feel of it. If the pupils are keen enough then they ought to be willing to get plenty of throwing practice in addition to the tennis lesson. Anyway, the proposition can be put to them.

Pupil Practice

1. Over-arm throwing and catching in pairs, across the net, or in any suitable formation. (A basic eye-training, co-ordination practice for several major games) Emphasise the correct throwing stance: semi-open/sideways, transferrence of weight, follow-through.
2. Throwing at ground targets. Place row of small hoops, numbered, across both right and left forecourts, class paired off across the net, positioned on *service lines* or as close to the net as may be necessary. From correct throwing stance, throw tennis balls at targets, partner receives and returns throw. Aim to score points by hitting inside the hoops (a facsimile of the aiming spot for the full serve).
3. Move back progressively towards baseline as aim and throwing style improves. Shorter pupils may never actually have much success from the baseline owing to the net obscuring the targets,* but this is unimportant. The main thing is to develop familiarity with the over-arm throwing action into the opposite forecourt, with specific aim, from the correct throwing stance (to be developed into the full service stance).

Time: 5 minutes.

---

*Some teachers advise lowering the net to accommodate very young, or short pupils.

Service and Smash

(2) *Place the ball and let it fall beginners' service*

This is special co-ordination training for the non-racket arm in placing the ball upwards above head-height, in the correct position to be struck by the racket-head, with its throwing action.

First ball released and placed above head-height with smooth stretch and firm wrist.

Second ball still held between palm and last two fingers. (Learn to separate the balls in your grip).

Follow-through with full arm and fingers stretch.

Racket arm raised and taken back to 'Shoulder serve' position as the ball is placed upwards (but not hit) in this practice.

Upper-body slightly rotated with weight-transferrence onto rear foot as ball is placed.

Ball allowed to drop to the ground, 'on target' into the small hoop placed just in front and to right of leading foot.

Body-weight more onto rear foot as the placing movement is performed.

Fig. 29. Placing the ball

NOTE: Get into the habit from the start of holding two balls in the left hand for placement: the first, held between ball of thumb and first two fingertips; the second between palm and last two fingers.

Line-up leading foot and shoulder in direction of intended throw (serve); front foot 4 in. behind baseline and to right of centre mark.

Have row of small hoops along front of baseline for class practice.

Tennis for Schools

(3) *Ball and racket up together beginners' service*

Starting from the *service line* and without the hoops; this will be the start of an identical movement to the previous one of placing the ball; only this time the ball is going to be hit across the net.

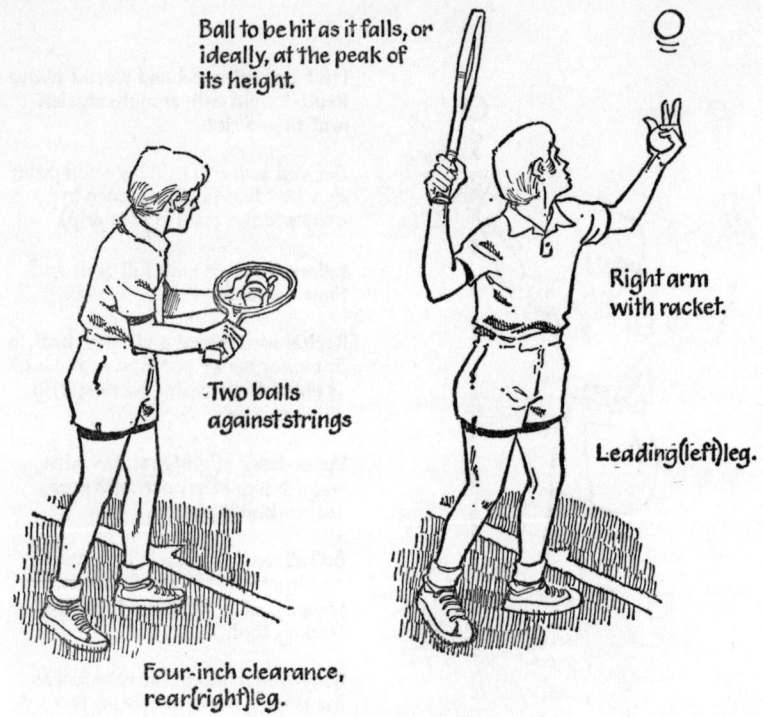

Fig. 30. Simple 'Shoulder Serve'

(1) Line-up feet and leading shoulder in 'Open stance' behind service line.
(2) Hold two balls in left hand, racket with 'Shake-hands' grip in right; racket-head on edge pointing across net (taking aim), balls held against strings; or racket lightly supported at throat.
(3) Raise racket and balls together from this 'Service' position, placing first ball up to be hit.
(4) This is the simplest of all over-head serving actions, with no preliminary backswing.

Service and Smash

(4) *Push or pat the ball beginners' service*

This is not a substitute for a good, full serve with preliminary 'back-scratcher' swing. But it is the simplest movement for a complete beginner to the service action. Once this co-ordination of placing the ball and simple over-head strike is achieved, starting from the service line, the pupil moves back, step-by-step towards the baseline, practising this easy shoulder serve. Two points: don't try for strength and velocity; concentrate on co-ordination and accuracy. The big serve will soon come.

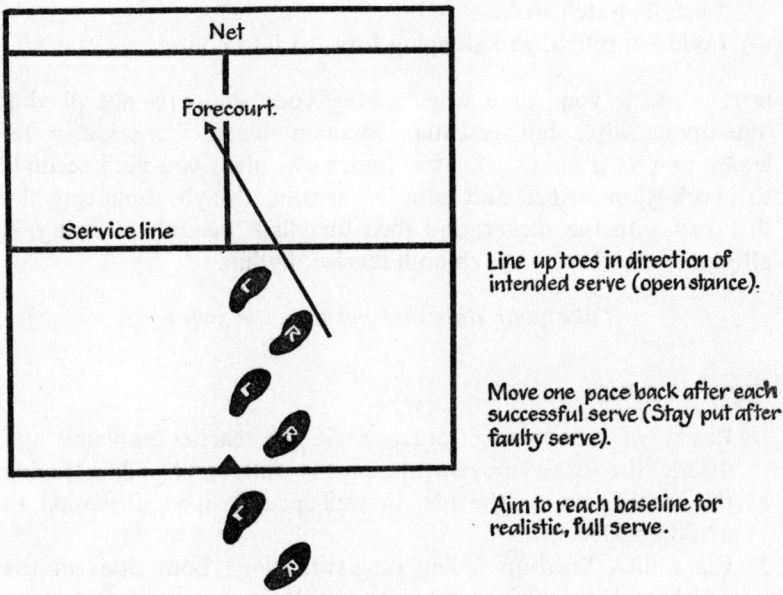

Fig. 31. 'Shoulder Serve' progression

With only the minimum (or no) backswing, push or pat the ball across the net into the diagonal service court.

Full Service (*throw: 'Cannon-ball' straight*)
Grip: 'Chopper'
Start: Service position (sideways/slightly open)

STROKE PRODUCTION:
(1) Taking the stance, your time, and aim – relaxed. Then first 'Pendulum' swing.
(2) Place the ball and into backswing and 'back-scratcher' position.
(3) 'Throw' the racket head at the ball as it begins to fall for full-stretch strike.
(4) Follow-through, and stepping forward into court.

NOTE: taking your time when taking your stance is not playing 'one-upmanship', but essential common sense. Consciously relaxing as you position your feet and body, gives you vital seconds to check your stance and ease the tension. Maybe bouncing the first ball with the racket, and then that first 'pendulum' swing, is all part of developing the smooth service rhythm.

Take your time and get into the swing.

Pupil Practice
1. Plenty of 'shadowing' practice as the teacher explains and details the basic movements of the full serve. Class facing the teacher across the net, in well-spaced, open formation to avoid accidents.
2. Class then lined-up facing outwards along both sides of the court, and encouraged to enjoy ample free practice at serving ('cannon-balling') into the side netting. Teacher moves along the lines, observing and offering corrective comment or compliments where indicated.
3. Class split equally across court, facing each other over the net; starting from the service line (especially if young pupils). Ad lib serving practice aiming at opposite diagonal forecourt. Use the 'moving back towards baseline' incentive (staying-put after faulty serves).

Service and Smash

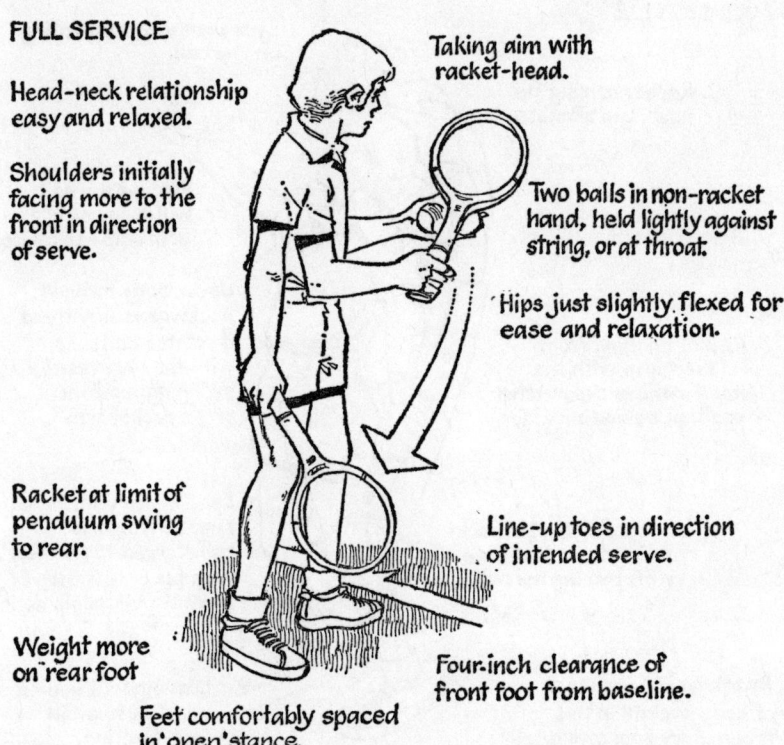

Fig. 32. (1) Service stance and 'Pendulum' swing

Tennis for Schools

FULL SERVICE

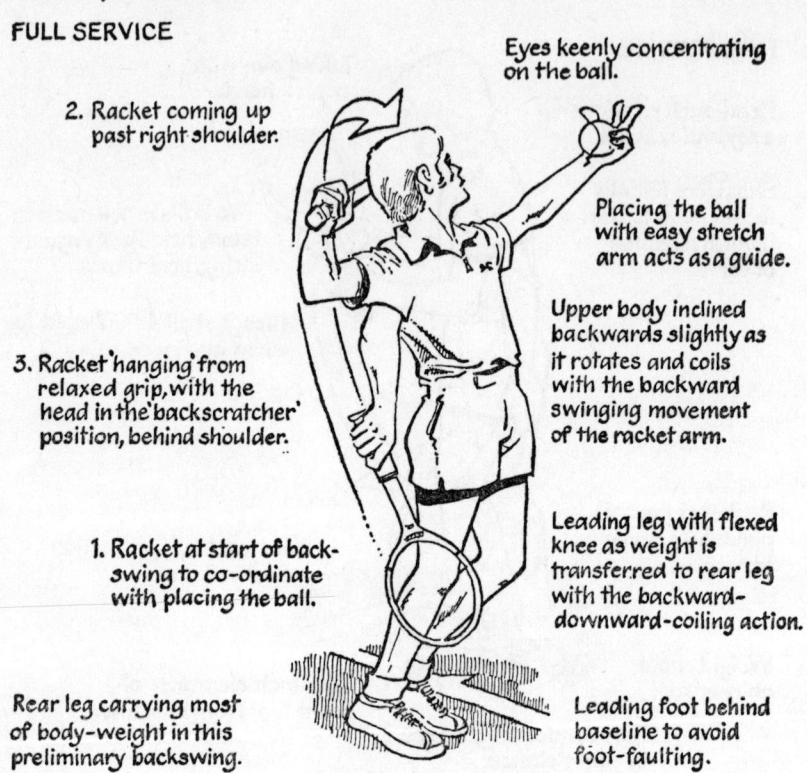

Fig. 33. (2) Placing the ball and backswing

NOTE: at the completion of the backswing (as the ball goes up), the 'chopper' grip is relaxed to allow the racket to 'hang' loosely near the centre of the back, pointing groundwards.

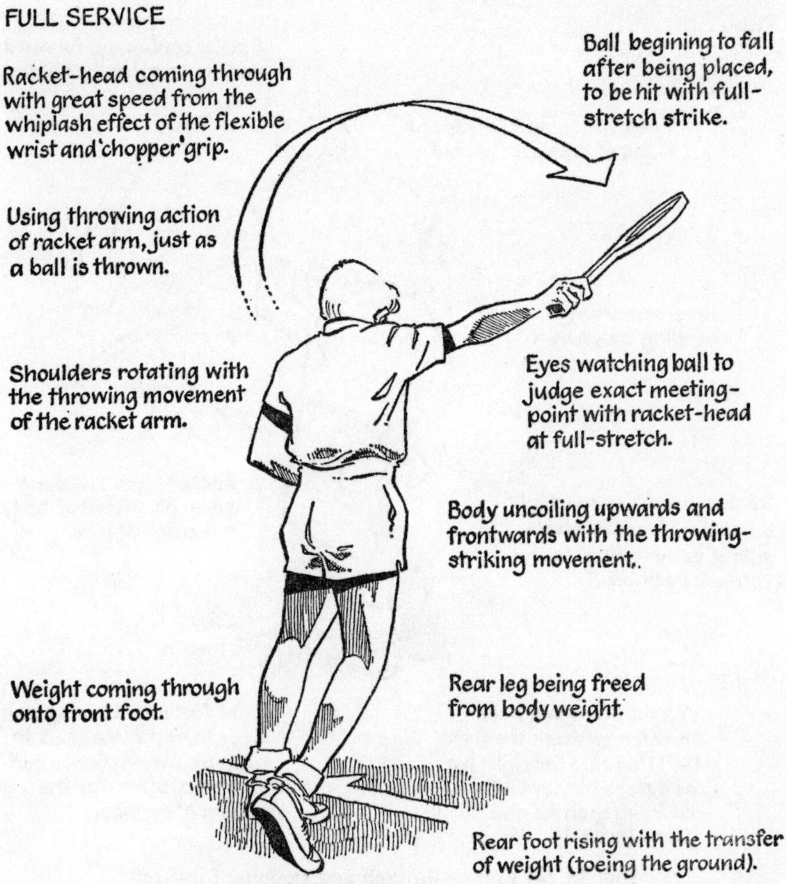

Service and Smash

FULL SERVICE

Racket-head coming through with great speed from the whiplash effect of the flexible wrist and 'chopper' grip.

Ball begining to fall after being placed, to be hit with full-stretch strike.

Using throwing action of racket arm, just as a ball is thrown.

Shoulders rotating with the throwing movement of the racket arm.

Eyes watching ball to judge exact meeting-point with racket-head at full-stretch.

Body uncoiling upwards and frontwards with the throwing-striking movement.

Weight coming through onto front foot.

Rear leg being freed from body weight.

Rear foot rising with the transfer of weight (toeing the ground).

Fig. 34. (3) 'Throwing' the racket head at the ball

NOTE: From the relaxed hanging, 'backscratcher' position of the racket behind the back, the grip is tightened to regain the 'chopper' grip and the racket swung upwards and forwards with a whiplash effect to strike the ball at full-stretch. Additional power is released by rotating the upper-body frontwards into the strike.

Tennis for Schools

FULL SERVICE

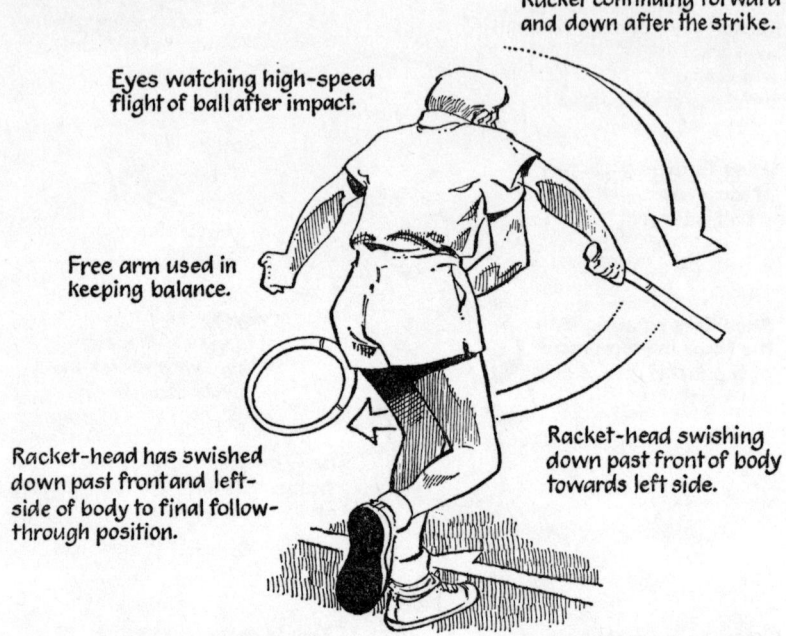

Racket continuing forward and down after the strike.

Eyes watching high-speed flight of ball after impact.

Free arm used in keeping balance.

Racket-head has swished down past front and left-side of body to final follow-through position.

Racket-head swishing down past front of body towards left side.

Weight has again been transferred from the front (left) leg onto the right leg as it steps forward into court *after* strike and follow through.

Right foot now leading as it steps forward into court to take-up over-balance and start the run-in for the return of service.

Fig. 35. (4) Follow-through and stepping forward

NOTE: Avoid just 'stepping-in' with the right foot until *after* impact with the ball and follow-through. If you step-in too soon you risk foot-faulting. The swing-in of the right leg after the strike is to take-up a new 'ready' position, or run-in towards the net.

If there is a tendency to step forward during the stroke itself (impact and follow-through), go back to the beginning and consciously keep both feet firmly on the ground throughout. This will correct faulty over-balance. Toeing the ground with the right foot is O.K.

Service and Smash

4. Actual target practice into small hoops or ball boxes can be introduced another time, once pupils have mastered the basic movement, rhythm and timing of the service action.

NOTE: Emphasise that there must be no forcing, nor use of excessive strength with these initial practices. The important factors are:

Concentration, Timing, Rhythm

Slice and topspin ('kicker') serves

Every player needs these additional weapons in his armoury. They are very functional, effective, even deadly, and can be

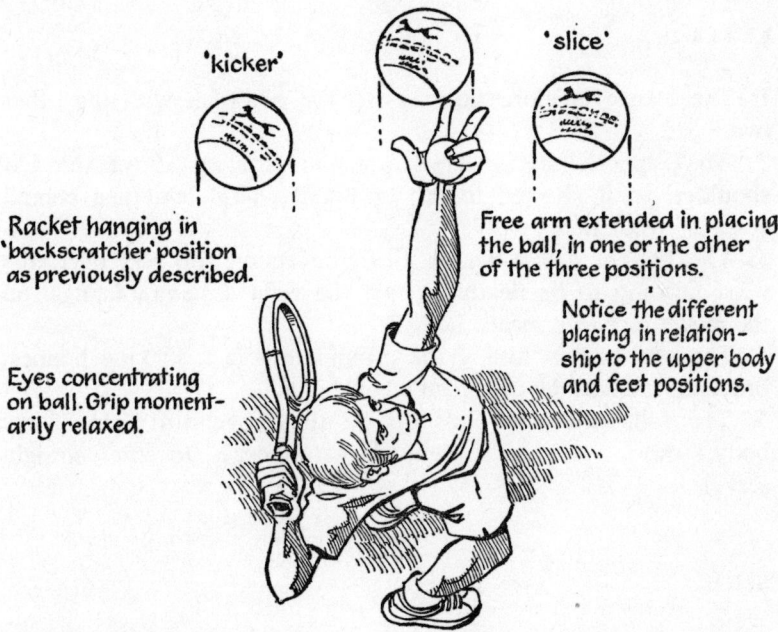

Fig. 36. Placing the ball for the 'slice, 'cannon-ball' and 'kicker'

Tennis for Schools

exciting and very satisfying to perform. Even so, beginners must not imagine they will learn to serve sliced, or 'kicker' aces simply by throwing the ball up off-centre. Practise on these is going to involve separate, concentrated and determined sessions. The conscious feel of the body in action with these two specialities is different and should not be introduced until *after* the straight (flat) 'cannon-ball' serve has been mastered.

Having said that, I'll illustrate a simple description of how the slice and the 'kicker' is achieved, enough to get you started, then leave you to develop the finer points as you need them.

KICKER

1. The stance is more sideways to the net than with the other two.
2. To help accurate placing, put the ball up above the left shoulder, so if allowed to fall un-hit, it would land just behind you near your heels.
3. The ball is struck with a brushing action, up and over, the wrist needing to be flexible to get the right amount of angle on the racket face as it meets the ball.
4. The effect upon hitting the ground is a fast, kicking bounce, breaking towards the opponent's backhand.
5. The follow-through ends up on the racket-arm side of the body, down past the right leg (opposite to the straight serve).

SLICE

1. The stance is the same as for the straight serve – sideways-to-open.
2. But by placing the ball more to the right of centre, this would fall to the right of your feet, if un-hit.
3. The striking action needs to be visualised and felt as brushing across the back of the ball, with *long contact* from left to right. This is the slicing movement, creating side-spin.

Service and Smash

4. The fact that the strings stay in contact longer with the slice, reduces velocity, but increases control: (the longer the ball stays with the strings, the better the control)
5. The follow-through is across the front of the body and down past the left side, the arm maybe not so fully extended.

NOTE: although I started with a cautious reminder about special effort needed to learn these additional serves, there is no argument they will have to be learnt. In fact, some coaches recommend that the slice be learnt first (before the straight serve), as it teaches more finesse, touch and control (as against simply smashing over 'cannon-balls' with a flat trajectory).

Admittedly, there is the risk of inadvertently encouraging brute force with the 'cannon-ball', even confusing it with the actual smash stroke.

Another thing: these flat trajectory serves may be better suited to the taller player, because being a flat serve, the action is all a matter of angles. Whereas, the 'kicker' with its topspin and the slice with its greater racket control, does enable the server to bring the ball down more sharply over the net into the opponent's forecourt, which is just what a shorter player needs to do.

The main thing is, master the basic action of the uncomplicated straight serve, then go on to learning the other two variations as soon as you feel confident and ready. All three have to be learnt in the long run.

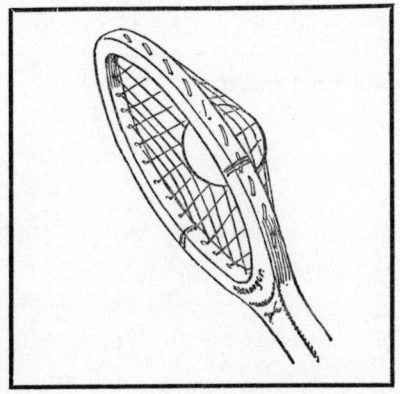

Fig. 37. Long contact. (Thinking of the racket strings reacting as a lacrosse stick – momentarily retaining the ball before slinging it. This effect applies more to the slice than to the straight serve

Tennis for Schools

The forehand (*overhead*) smash (*throw: direct angled*)

Grip: 'Chopper'.

Start: Seldom fixed, nearly always mobile; but sideways-on, left shoulder towards net (similar to serving).

STROKE PRODUCTION:
(1) Watch and move under the falling ball – sideways-on.
(2) Left arm points at the ball; racket goes straight back over the shoulder – no wind-up.
(3) 'Throw' the racket head at full stretch (jump if you must) to get it above the ball.
(4) Weight flows forward. Watch point of impact. Shoulders turn and follow-through.

NOTE: although similar to the serve, don't confuse the two. The smash is a highly mobile, dynamic shot calling for very active footwork. Be quick to get forward or back, underneath the falling ball – *sideways-on*. And never take your eyes off it. This needs quick-footed confidence and determination to attack.

Experience is the teacher to help you decide whether to smash a high lob from the sky, or let it bounce first before putting it away. Bounces can be best for beginners.

Vary your shots from smashing hard and deep into your opponent's court, to using tactical placement with deceptive angles.

Variety can often beat speed.

Service and Smash

THE FOREHAND SMASH (OVERHEAD)

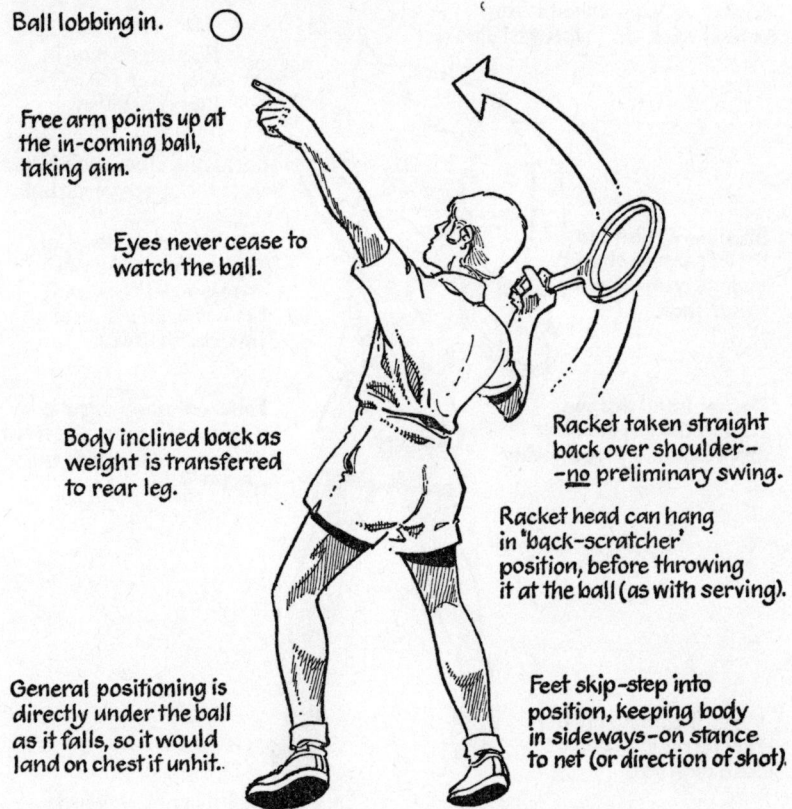

Fig. 38. Getting set for the 'Smash'

NOTE: lots of practice is needed in moving forwards or backwards fast, with nimble skip-steps, while maintaining body sideways-on to net.

'Running' backwards while watching the in-coming ball is also a necessary skill. However you move to get into position to meet the ball, *turn your head to keep your eyes on it*.

Full stretch for the strike, with racket head in advance of the hand upon impact, to bring the ball sharply down, either bullet direct, or angled to a corner.

Jumping to smash high lobs is the next step to learn after you've learnt good smashes with your feet firmly on the ground.

Tennis for Schools

THE BACKHAND SMASH

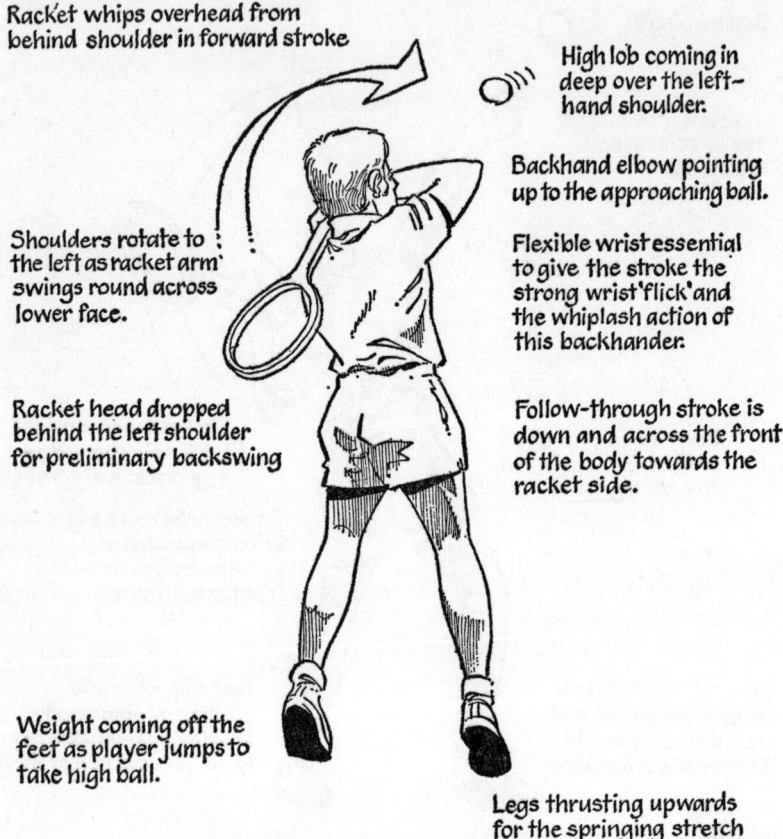

Fig. 39. Special stance for the 'Backhand Smash'

NOTE: this is a stylish and spectacular, but weaker stroke, which nevertheless has to be made sometimes, such as responding to a high, deep lob to the left backcourt. This could be too difficult to run around and try to take with the forehand.

Pupil Practice

1. Deal with the forehand overhead first. The backhand smash is not designed for weak muscles and delicate wrists. But it can come, with strength training.
2. 'Shadow' the stroke with the class briefly, to impress the differences between the smash and the serve.
   * No wind-up backswing; racket taken straight back.
   * Free arm points at the in-coming ball as a sight.
   * Body moves into position in a sideways-on stance.
   * Feet need to be nimble and sure to skip-step the body into its striking position under the ball.
3. Pupils practise moving adroitly about the court with this skipping, sideways movement. Lots of 'running' backwards while watching imaginary in-coming high lob (be careful of accidents).
4. Class lined-up facing side netting with racket and six balls each pupil. Free practice at throwing up own balls to smash. Teacher careful to check and correct any tendency to 'serve' the ball instead of smash.
5. Class paired-off in opposite courts: feed (by hand) high balls for partner to smash. Actual lobbing by racket can be introduced as soon as individual pupils are judged ready for it.

   Time: 5 minutes plus.

14

Volleys and Half-volleys

Volleys can be easier than groundstrokes. Confidence will make it so. Volleys are most certainly essential strokes which every player can learn to perform well – some become volley specialists and create the impression of being terrors of the court. They needn't be. It all depends upon how they are handled.

I'm simply saying, keep a sense of proportion. Tennis doesn't have to be reduced to serving, rushing and volleying. And although some players (not necessarily the top ones) do like to have us believe that tennis is all smash and slam, this would do a great disservice to the game. It has far and away greater range, artistry and finesse than that, and we must advance this promotion of the finer skills. Volleying is part of our repertoire of these exciting skills.

The forehand volley (punch or block)

Grip: 'Shake-hands' (beginners); 'Chopper' (advanced).

Start: 'Predator' stance (low); or mobile.

STROKE PRODUCTION:
(1) Watch and ready.
(2) Step across with shoulder turn, racket up with bent elbow. *No* backswing.
(3) Brace the wrist, punch the racket head through the ball.
(4) Long contact, follow-through with body-weight going forward.

Volleys and Half-volleys

THE HIGH, ATTACKING VOLLEY

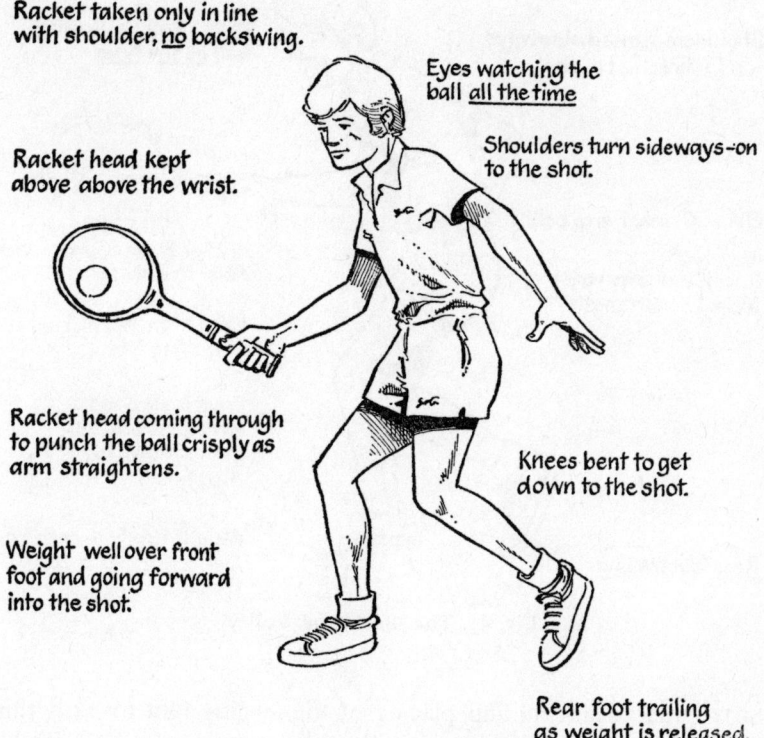

Fig. 40. The 'Forehand Volley'

NOTE: for incoming balls above net height, punch flat and down, with slightly closed racket face. Hit hard and go for placement.

Balls below net height require some backspin from an open racket face, gaining extra control by long contact and punching *under* the ball (don't confuse this with under-cutting).

Keep the racket head well cocked and try to take the ball out in front and a foot or so to the side. Be prepared to stretch for wider balls.

Tennis for Schools

THE BACKHAND VOLLEY

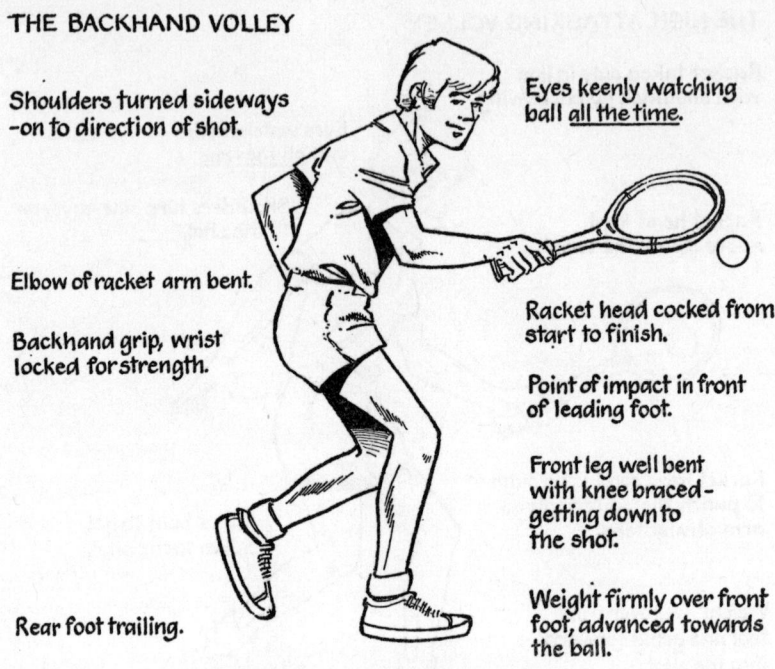

Fig. 41. The 'Backhand Volley'

NOTE: the advancing and placing of the leading foot towards this shot, along with the sideways shoulder turn, make this stroke effective. The height of the approaching ball decides how much the leading knee shall be bent.

Be prepared and willing to bend the knees and go in very deep to low volleys, keeping the racket head cocked and the wrist solidly locked. This virtually changes them into waist-high volleys, which is the champions' way of making this stroke. There is no excuse for laziness.

Volleys and Half-volleys

THE HALF-VOLLEY – Forehand
Backhand

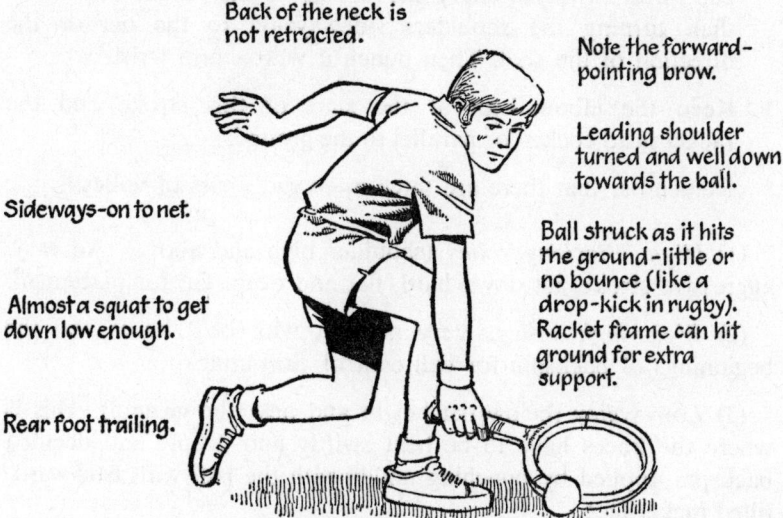

The head-neck relationship is important with this stroke; keep in mind the idea leading with the brow and so avoid constriction in the neck vertebrae.

Back of the neck is not retracted.

Note the forward-pointing brow.

Leading shoulder turned and well down towards the ball.

Sideways-on to net.

Almost a squat to get down low enough.

Ball struck as it hits the ground – little or no bounce (like a drop-kick in rugby). Racket frame can hit ground for extra support.

Rear foot trailing.

Fig. 42. The 'Half-volley'

NOTE: like it or not, the knees have to be bent deeply with this shot, to get the racket head parallel to the ground.

Often a defensive, reflex shot played in no-man's-land. Nevertheless, go well and deeply into it, striking the ball the *instant* it leaves the ground. Don't hesitate.

A *push touch* stroke with long contact.

Special points about the volleys

* Never be nervous of volleys. Go into them with attacking confidence, then they can be easier than drives.

* Think of the action as putting out your hand to catch the ball, with no preliminary movement of the racket arm other than turning the shoulders sideways-on to the net or the direction of the shot. Then punch it with a firm wrist.

* Keep the elbow bent at the start of this stroke and the racket head cocked or parallel to the ground.

* Remember that there are three main categories of volleys:

(1) *High, attacking volley* (shoulder high and above). An easy, aggressive stroke, hit down hard, flat and deep. Go for placement.

(2) *Waist-high volley*. Very natural, with bent knees and the beginnings of backspin for ball control. Still attacking.

(3) *Low volley* (below net height and near the ground). This is where the knees have to be bent swiftly and deeply and decided backspin applied by punching underneath the ball with backward-tilted racket face.

* Don't overdo the backward tilt, or the backspin will become undercutting and the ball will lose too much speed. Think of *blocking* with backward tilt, not cutting. The object is to lift the ball safely over the net.

* If you have to volley almost by reflex and there's no time to get your feet into position for the classic stroke, give it a hip sway and a twist to bring the shoulders round to make the shot. Otherwise, it will have to be played square-on to the net – as an emergency, blocking stroke.

* Watch the ball and read the play at all times, then there should be very little need for 'emergency', off-the-cuff shots.

* Never be afraid to play the *backhand volley*. The backhand grip and stroke is ideally strong for the volley, with a naturally stylish action. Let your confidence flow into the stroke – it will want to.

Volleys and Half-volleys

* Aim to play volleys close to the net, to catch them at their highest peak and *punch them down*.
* Play the volleys with your weight flowing forward on to the front foot.
* The longer contact made for low volleys turn them into push and touch shots, with control more important than speed.
* The backhand volley needs lots of shadow practice to get the *feel and image* of the stroke firmly built-in to the nervous and muscular systems.
* The backhand volley is too high to punch with a locked wrist when it can't be reached without jumping – this would then become the backhand smash with flexible wrist.
* Walls are wonderful for practising volleys – left side (backhand), right side (forehand). Use them for individual and small group practices at every opportunity.

Play volleys well inside the service court.

Pupil Practice

Volleying requires a firm grip, quick reflexes, an attacking spirit, plenty of confidence and the need to be fast about the court. You'll be lucky if you get this all at once with beginners. They have to build it up gradually; but if they are too timid, they'll lose the essential volley dash and style. Yet if pushed too hard too soon, they'll most likely misjudge their shots, mishit their strokes and get discouraged by too many wildly-hit balls – so will the ball boys! So practices have to allow for this.

1. *Teaching to eliminate backswing.* Pairs: one line backed-up against the side-netting (the strikers), partners (the feeders) facing 10 paces into court. Feeding (underarm) to striker's forehand side, shoulder high: volley back to feeder – FEED – VOLLEY – CATCH. Repeat until forehand volley is developing nicely, then change to backhand. When this is learnt, switch to feeding alternate sides for quick reaction and grip-changing practice. NOTE: being close to side-netting restricts

Tennis for Schools

the backswing, which is necessary. Feeding by hand provides greater accuracy for the earlier practices, also necessary.

2. *Wall volleying (forehand – backhand).* Individuals or pairs. This often keeps the odd man out busy and is most valuable. The individual has to keep his own alternate sides supplied rhythmically (after he has mastered each side in turn). Partners can feed each other off the wall, changing sides frequently to practise their forehand and backhand strokes.

3. *Volleying in pairs.* Doesn't have to be over the net to start with; more pupils can be accommodated along the side-netting, facing each other across court, but with one line down the centre to be closer to their partners, to reduce mis-hits. Later, they can rally to each other across the centre net, no further back than from the service lines. As they improve, this volley rallying can develop into pattern volleying to teach accuracy and ball control. Pupils numbered-off into groups of four, facing 2 by 2 across the net. Keep a volley rally going in the pattern of $1-3-2-4-1$ *ad infinitum.*

Time: 10 minutes.

NOTE: Just a few of the many varied practices you can organise the pupils into, referred to in Part Three; the basic principle being to select one or two key skills for training in each lesson, with variety, fun, interest and performance in mind.

15
The Lobs

If your opponent seems to dominate the net and you can't make a successful passing shot, lift the ball over his head to his backcourt, as close to his baseline as you dare! This could require nerve. But that's the lob. A most useful, in fact necessary weapon in your armoury of big guns.
Forehand-backhand GRIP, FOOTWORK, STANCE, STROKE – as with groundstrokes (almost).

Flat hit, attacking lob

* Use a shorter, lifted swing, to loft the ball just clear of an opponent's up-stretched racket at the height of his jump at the net.

* Watch the ball keenly to play it off the centre of the strings, feeling it as a touch shot with long contact.

* Get a feeling of lift in the forward and upward swing, with a straight-arm follow-through, pointing the racket forward and up.

* Aim deeply to the far baseline, preferably to the opponent's backhand side, forcing him to use the weaker backhand smash (if he can get there).

Topspin lob

* Turn the wrist over to the left as you contact the ball, brushing the racket face up and over. This will produce topspin – sometimes called a 'rolled' topspin.

* Follow-through comes down lower, with the racket-head pointing more to the ground.

* The idea of this topspin is to get extra control from the ball and make it shoot away after bouncing and more difficult to return.

Backspin lob (*defensive*)

* Push the racket-head through underneath the ball, with an open-face; but limited follow-through upwards.
* This backspin technique takes the pace out of a powerful incoming shot, controls the contact, holds the ball longer in the air and causes it to fall more vertically.
* But remember, it is a defensive stroke, parrying an attacking shot to allow you more time to regain position.
* Lob high enough to gain that extra time to recover, especially to be prepared to defend your court against the following smash – which you'll get if you lob short.
* You don't swing at this backspin shot, but get the power in your push at the ball from straightening the racket elbow.

NOTE: by forcing a dominant opponent to continually run back to defend his own backcourt, the accurately-placed lob can give you breathing-space, while helping to tire him out, you hope. But don't misjudge him: if your lob is timid or weak, he will most likely make good capital out of it by smashing the return for a kill, especially if you set your shot up for a kill by slowing down the flight by too much under-slicing.

It's up to you to perfect these lobs (or as near as possible) so that you can use them selectively, aggressively and with devastating accuracy. If you're not prepared to put in the practice to do this, then you're asking for trouble, because a timid, unsure lobber is a sitting duck to an aggressive and experienced opponent. Ask yourself often, are your lobs worth the effort? The answer surely must be yes. Practice makes precision.

Pupil Practice

Space is at a premium here, because you are encouraging high, long shots and smashing returns. Early beginners may not be able to control their rackets well enough to make the best use of limited space. Wildly hit balls (not intentional) can be expected,

The Lobs

but not tolerated for long! This is where controlled feeding, first by hand, then by racket is so useful.

1. *Ball sense training.* Pairs: lined-up facing at opposite baselines. Simple throwing target practice. High, over-arm throwing to place ball at distant partner's feet just in front of baseline (this is to develop an early appreciation of the distance). Partner gathers after first bounce and makes return throw.
2. *Throwing lobs.* Pairs: a progression of the above. One row line-up along baseline, with the balls; partners lined-up along *service* line. High throw over partner's head, aiming at far baseline; partner turns quickly, runs to gather the ball on first bounce, turns to stay at baseline ready to make return throw to first partner who meanwhile, has run forward to take position inside service line, etc., and etc.
3. *Lobbing and recovering with rackets.* Pairs: a further progression with rackets. Just as No. 2, but using rackets to feed and return the ball. Realistic practice at lobbing and placing over partner's head (and above his reach), with following return feed after first bounce near the baseline, etc.
4. *Lob and smash.* Pairs: two lines, one *outside* side-netting, 10 to 20 feet away; partners facing, same distance *inside* court. So the side-netting now divides the two lines of partners. Outside partner lobs ball over the netting, inside partner smashes return shot into the netting: (a piece of paper wedged into the wire can be the target for the smasher) Lines change sides. This is a very safe practice (always providing there is sufficient spacing between individual smashers). Of course, it presupposes that there is plenty of spare space surrounding the courts.
5. *Lob and smash variation.* Similar practice to above, but a variation can be organised using volleyball nets, or rope strung between tall posts. Object: lob ball over rope to partner, who smashes return underneath the rope back to first partner. Or any variation you care to devise.

Time: 10 minutes.

NOTE: as you would expect, there are dozens of enjoyable practices to be devised, or borrowed from other teachers' experiences.

16

Touch Shot Volleys: Lob, Drop, Stop

Here we enter the world of special strokes for improving players. If we thought of the aforegoing strokes as 'Big Guns', then these ensuing shots are from essential 'small arms' fire. They have to be learnt by anyone with more than half a mind to treat his or her tennis seriously and add additional finesse and artistry to their game, for the mutual enjoyment of player and spectator alike.

These shots require the ability to feel the ball *on the strings*. That's why they are called touch shots. This is where that oft repeated phrase in tennis comes into its own: LONG CONTACT. These are the vital ingredients:

* read the play and decide the stroke in advance.
* start your own stroke in time to perform it with an attitude of correctness and freedom from panic.
* watch the ball from your opponent's racket to your own. 'Developing a good eye for a ball.'
* aim to contact the ball in the centre of your strings.
* try to feel it in contact there as long as you can (remember the lacrosse stick image?). This is flattening the ball against your strings. It gives you that extra ball control.
* Throughout your practising and playing keep reminding yourself about long contact.

Now to develop super control over the motor muscles of your racket arm and to command their sensitive response – for TOUCH SHOTS. Basically, they mean retaining the ball in contact with

Touch Shot Volleys: Lob, Drop, Stop

your racket strings, long enough for you to impart your intention to it *wilfully;* then follow through the stroke as if part of you were actually following and guiding the flight of the ball. Remember the two opposing types of shots: (1) where you strike at the ball and it bounces off your racket-head as if rebounding from a piece of hardboard – the very antipathy of 'touch'. (2) where you feel and guide the ball with your racket strings with long and sensitive contact. Your aim is to make No. 2 your style of play – the Ille Nastase style.

Lob volley (*punch*)

Used against a dominant opponent at the net. Instead of trying to aim your return volley as a passing shot, try to clear his upstretched racket by converting your volley to a lob. You will force him away from the net to run and retrieve this lob-volley from the backcourt and give yourself time to think what to do with his return, if he makes it.

Approach the shot as you would for a normal volley, but with enough open-face on the strings to create strong backspin, by punching through the ball with the whole arm and stiff wrist – keeping this *very firm*. The follow-through will be longer, guiding the ball to his backcourt.

The element of surprise is valuable, so disguise your intention as you approach this shot. Only you should have prior knowledge that you intend to lift the ball over his head.

Drop volley (*block*)

Requires a delicate touch and nice sense of timing, because you've got to literally drop that ball exactly where you want it. A return shot used on slow balls, with sharp underspin and no follow-through, aiming to drop the ball dead short over the net, stranding your opponent unprepared at the back of the court this time. A completely opposite reaction from the lob volley.

Block, don't punch at this shot, getting the maximum, clinging-to-the-strings feeling from the ball as you use your fingers to manipulate the racket and softly apply underspin. At the same time, take more pace off the approaching ball by pulling back the racket at the instant of impact.

This is definitely a stroke you use when close to the net yourself, with your opponent near, on or behind his own baseline. This is where you want to embarrass him, and where you can dominate the net for a change – always assuming you haven't advertised your intention in advance.

Stop volley (touch and block)

Perhaps there isn't much left to say about this touch shot variation. I'm not recommending that you push it on to raw beginners. They've enough technique to learn without having their muscle responses complicated any more by way-out strokes that are the speciality of the artist. However, our encouragement lies in the certain knowledge that they will eventually want to get on to these remaining shots once they are feeling pleased with their basic strokes.

The *stop volley* is a shot they ought to have up their sleeve, so introduce it when you judge them to be capable of applying the special racket and ball sense required.

This stroke is to take the pace off fast on-coming balls, and it would be foolish to attempt it from anywhere but up close to the net. Block the on-coming ball with a delicate sense of touch, a slightly open-face to impart undespin, and a sharp, sensitive withdrawal of the racket head at the precise split-second of impact.

The combination of these skills should kill the ball's speed and allow it to be dropped precisely just over the net and out of your opponent's reach – unless he's a superb scrambler.

Once this skill is learnt, then enrich it by adding precise placement to your return – direct it low over the net towards the sides of the court away from your opponent. This is when the player becomes the artist.

Pupil Practice

Because the stop volley requires delicacy of touch and is a stroke of great finesse, pupils ought to appreciate the need for concentrated, special practice. *Their* encouragement lies in the knowledge that they have the ability to produce this spectacular little shot by doing these practices.

Touch Shot Volleys: Lob, Drop, Stop

1. *Exaggerated underspin:* (making the ball spin and bounce sharply backwards) Two lines of partners, *feeders* and *strikers*, facing (any field, playground or court space judged suitable).
   (a) 20 ft. apart for first practice;
   (b) Regulation, baseline-to-baseline as skill improves.
   Feeder throws or hits a nice controlled ball to bounce in front of his partner. Striker, by going in and down to the ball, underspins it sharply to make it continue its bounce towards the netting behind him. *This is learning to underspin the ball.* Partners interchange frequently.
2. *Vertical underspin:* (making the ball spin sharply and fly vertically upwards) Pupil formation as for No. 1. Feeder throws or hits a controlled ball to bounce in front of partner, who uses less underspin this time, sends it vertically into the air and tries to catch it with his left hand without moving his position. Return ball to feeder. Partners interchange.
3. *Underspin forward:* (making the ball spin and rebound forward) Pupil formation on court, baseline-to-baseline facing in pairs. Feeder sends the ball down-court as before, striker goes in and down to perform *touch shot* with underspin, trying to drop the ball forward:
   (a) into his own service square;
   (b) dropping it nearer to the net;
   (c) then finally just over the net.

NOTE: these practices must be converted to DROP and STOP volleys, once the basic dropshot skill is learnt; in which case, the partners must approach closer to the net so the strikers can make their strokes from there as previously described.

4. *Dropshot and recovery rally.* This stimulates both the actual dropshot and its recovery between partners. Formation in pairs, two lines facing on opposite sides of the net.
   No. 1 feeds across easily to his opposite partner, who returns with a dropshot back to No. 2 in the first line, who tries to dropshot it back again, and so on, to and fro down the line. Continue until the rally breaks down.

Time: 10 minutes.

Tennis for Schools

NOTE: if this form of practice reveals weaknesses (like causing pupils to be inactive, or proving too difficult as a rally), variations can be used. The original intention of teaching the DROP and STOP volley, may well be too difficult as a rally – yet at the same time, we want pupils to sharpen-up and develop quick responses.

17

Other Specialised Touch Shots: Slice, Cut, Chop, Chip

All four strokes are made to produce underspin and are opportunity, convenience or safety shots. When made with a longish action and long contact they are 'slices'; when the action is restricted with a sharp, short cutting movement they are 'cuts'. If this is done heavily it's a 'chop'. If you advance tigerishly to the ball, cut and move in to the net, this is called a 'chip-approach'.

So there you have it. Not difficult shots to perform, mainly because you don't have to make long-winded preparation, like full-blooded, looped swings. On the contrary, they are handy little surprise shots, popped out of the bag when there isn't time for anything else. But although of restricted action, they do have long contact, so you can claim that extra degree of control with them.

But remember, they are not fast, passing shots against an opponent dominating the net, because they are slower and tend to hang in the air, easy meat for an alert volleyer. He'll have to be forced (or persuaded) back with a lob of sorts, before you pop one of these surprise underspins over the net and make him scramble for it. Fun and surprise? The game's full of it.

The slice

Can be either forehand or backhand, but is stronger and more effective on the backhand. The *backhand slice* is a deliberately and most useful defensive stroke against fast balls and as an approach shot to the net, especially as the underspin makes it stay low and skid, turn or shoot through on landing. Another valuable use for it is in the *recovery* stroke against a ball that

Tennis for Schools

has got past you and needs to be pulled back into play. This needs a strong yet flexible wrist, generally asking too much of young, weak beginners (A strong case for fitness training).

With the standard backhand grip, restrict the backswing so that instead of completing a loop, bring the racket-head directly downward and forward underneath the approaching ball. Have the racket-face open or back-tilted to glide it under the ball with a brushing action on impact. The angle of tilt must vary according to the height of the ball as it is struck.

(a) *High balls:* continue the follow-through downward as if to pull the ball down with the racket-face.

(b) *Low balls:* swish or swoop the racket-face underneath the ball as if to lift it.

(c) *Side-spin variation:* bring this in too for extra long contact control, by drawing the strings across the ball from left to right during the downward-forward action.

Plenty of experiment with these three techniques, and learn to get that feeling of *holding* and *guiding* the ball with the tilt and movement of the racket-face.

NOTE: to use this slice in the recovery shot, which is really an emergency stroke to pull back a ball that has gone past your normal striking position, loosen the wrist, reach back with a flicking movement and the sliced action to bring the ball back under control. You should be able to take the pace off it this way.

The cut, chop and chip

Handy as these emergency shots are, they are no substitute for good, honest forehand and backhand drives. Yet there are players (not first class) who slash, cut, chop and chip away at practically any type of shot. They have developed this style of play, but not for the best reasons. You have seen them. They don't get far this way.

I'm saying this to confirm your own low opinion of this kind of compensatory stroke-making. It can often be the outcome of deficient technique and failing to read the play, plus lack of genuine incentive. Perhaps I haven't quite put my finger on it even now. But I'm not condemning these 'convenience' shots, only registering a formal caution.

Other Specialised Touch Shots:

Let them be learnt. Get the pupils to 'play around with them', but never to get lazy in their execution. Each of these strokes requires the performer to pay strict attention to his footwork, stance and stroke-play, to his approach, grip, swing (or non-swing), angle of racket-face, strike and follow-through.

Each stroke has its own character and dignity. So bring them into the repertoire, but with respect – and caution. Always remember the cut, chop and chip are *convenience, opportunity* and *emergency* shots, not strong, basic foundation strokes.

If they can be mastered, then used in an *attacking* sense, as deliberate, calculated weapons, rather than purely defensively, then they really will add strength, aggressiveness and panache to a player's performance. We recognise top players who are capable of doing just this. They are hard to beat and a joy to watch.

When to use the chip

* When there isn't time for a full drive, or when the opponent has been returning with interest all the full groundstokes you can produce.
* To catch out an opponent who has been standing back.
* To angle your return across an opponent's body and break-up his playing rhythm, especially if he has been keeping you at bay.
* This is particularly effective against players who love to apply speed and pressure – the serve and volley types; or alternatively, against one-pace plodders.

Pupil Practice

Basically, they want opportunity to 'play around' with these strokes, but not to treat them casually or carelessly. It's mastery of the racket-face they need through grip and finger control. So plenty of TOUCH SHOT practice and experience at manipulating the racket-face by experimenting with tilt, types of swing and follow-through.

It's a matter of them finding out what effect their rackets can have on the ball with basic underspin technique similar to Chapter 13), then to experiment with the cut, chop and chip variations.

Tennis for Schools

NOTE: in earlier chapters on strokes I introduced *biodynamics*. I haven't plugged away at it relentlessly, but would like you to remind pupils from time-to-time of the necessity for their awareness of body-movement and how it effects their performance.

With these later specialised touch shots for example, the performer must be even more aware of using his body mechanism correctly:

* the foot placement towards the approaching ball.
* the even distribution of body-weight.
* the 'leading with the brow' and the forward inclination of the leading shoulder.
* the recovery of posture after the stroke and the resumption of the 'Predator' stance.
* and throughout, the keen sense of occupying space gracefully, combined with an awareness of delicacy of touch.

So I hope I haven't given the impression of being over-critical about those specialised shots. In fact, they should be invaluable for developing the biodynamic qualities that can turn the mediocre performer into an artist.

Just don't confuse them with the off-the-cuff, *reaction* (reflex) stroke I mentioned earlier. This is not a stroke to be classified and learnt. It's something a person is either born with or he isn't. There are only a few such performers with this natural flair in each generation. I doubt if a regular P.E. class would over-populate this field. But don't let me deter you.

18

Scrambling

It has been called 'the art of retrieving difficult or impossible balls'. Some star players have been outstandingly spectacular and successful at just this. They seem to possess that miraculous ability to reach and return any shot, no matter how tricky, powerful or seemingly a winner it may be. These incredibly quick-off-the-mark 'scramblers' always get their racket to the ball. It exasperates their opponents of course; but the spectators love it, they soon get to expect their heroes to do it every time. It becomes an essential part of the star quality. It certainly indicates superb fitness.

But, I must be honest and register one little negative observation. I'm not sure I care for the actual expression to 'scramble', as to scramble implies hurriedly trying to recover from an off-balance situation. You are trying to recover from being outfoxed by an unexpected return. You are caught 'on the wrong foot', or 'caught on the hop'. Or perhaps you have been 'caught napping'? Could it be that you failed to 'read the play'? So the end result is that you 'scramble' to retrieve. That is, if you care enough about your game, possess an indomitable will and an unshakable determination to play every shot.

Thinking about it like this and I must admit, 'scrambling' in this context of playing every shot, never giving up, is just the games spirit I would like to see motivating our youngsters – and not only in tennis; the will to strive, to do well (or even better than before), must be the bedrock of all sports. So unless you can think up a better word to describe this 'art of retrieving impossible balls', maybe we should we should go along with it – use it, encourage it, promote it with that 'gleam in the eye' approach that separates the teaching enthusiasts from the 'baby-minders'!

Getting players to scramble

Simply telling – or yelling is not necessarily going to motivate pupils to 'go after those difficult shots...' Two main factors make all the difference:

1. The need to enjoy the game.
2. The need to be in top physical condition.

So in both these areas we can recognise a responsibility. We do all we can to help our pupils enjoy the game, the learning and training as well as the playing for fun; and we present physical fitness to them in such a way that they really do begin to see it as not only something they must have, but as an essential quality they can't afford to be without. Is there any aspect of teaching where the teacher's personal example and leadership doesn't profoundly affect pupils' attitude and application?

1. How to stimulate pupils to enjoy their tennis?
2. How to get them to want to be fit?
3. How to get them to move? ('They stand like trees growing roots, waving their arms in the breeze' complained one P.E. teacher to me).
4. How to encourage them to treat their practices seriously, with concentration and determination?
5. How to motivate them to *care enough to make the effort?*

Finding teaching answers to these fundamental questions can result in the end product of *good* scrambling, which is one factor in the performance of a tennis player that is admired most – the spirit of not giving in, but to play every stroke with equal determination and effort. Which of course, is showing your respect for your opponent too and helping him to participate in an enjoyable game.

Warning players not to rely upon scrambling

Whatever the merits of scrambling, my underlying note of caution still holds good. Playing in haste produces a makeshift, defensive stroke and failure to get into a correct, attacking stroke position. Much of this is linked with the need to 'read the play' and the need to make the effort.

Scrambling

Thinking ahead of your stroke gives you extra dominance and confidence in selecting the kind of stroke you decide is best for the return shot.

It keeps you continuously on top of your game, like an alert car driver on a busy street – selecting his gears, using his pedals and caressing his wheel to suit the gradient and the occasion or emergency (A good driver has fewer emergencies and so doesn't rely on his reflexes to get him out of difficult or dangerous situations).

A good player who thinks ahead of his stroke also doesn't rely upon his reflexes to get him out of tricky court situations.

So now we ask players to settle in their minds the essential difference between 'thinking ahead of the stroke' and 'scrambling' to retrieve a shot that they had failed to anticipate or 'read' in advance.

Even so, the ability and willingness to scramble is a quality any self-respecting tennis player should be able to demonstrate – for both his own and his opponent's sake. Scrambling for that 'impossible' shot may win you the point, but the very fact that you made the effort is one of the many compliments you pay your opponent during a game, even if he loses it. It's no virtue or praise to him if he wins against a listless opponent – whom you wouldn't want to be you.

And I hope I haven't confused the issue here by seeming to be contradictory: on one hand admiring players who demonstrate their willingness and energy to scramble, and on the other, warning against relying upon scrambling as a substitute for thinking ahead. It occurs to me that there are two interpretations of scrambling. It depends upon your attitude. Meanwhile, combine sound, instinctive strokes with determined scrambling.

The 'secret' of scrambling

To learn how to scramble more effectively, these positive points should be practised at all age levels:

* *Early preparation* of strokes.
* Decide early upon the forehand or backhand side to which the ball is coming (or going to come).

SCRAMBLING

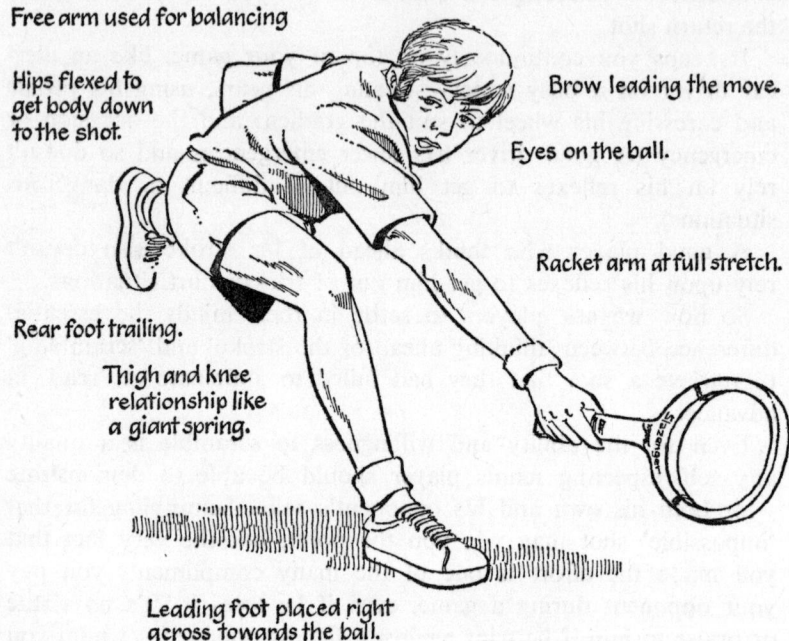

Fig. 43. Scrambling for difficult shots

This is part of star quality: principally the complete willingness and capability to go after and stoop low for shots. Notice how the player goes right in with the leading foot and well down with the knees. But often in scrambling, if you're caught unawares, there isn't time to make the correct, 'classic' moves, and the return shot has to be made from whatever foot and body position you find yourself in upon reaching the ball. I'm not condoning this, simply making the observation. Perhaps scrambling indicates that our star player is energetically human after all.

Scrambling

* Take advance action with the racket by getting it back early.
* Concentrate on the ball during the time the opponent's racket is travelling to meet it.
* Try to anticipate ('read') direction of the ball in advance, by concentrating on it just before and after impact by opponent's racket – the 'zip zone'.
* Develop ability to 'read' this impact direction by studying opponent's movement habits – foot placements, head and shoulder postures, angle of free hand and arm.

All this trains the player to quicken reaction and response, so saving seconds and getting (scrambling) to the ball more effectively.

Further reading and study: (particularly for stroke production)
Play Better Tennis with Tony Mottram (Stanley Paul, London, 1971). 50p.
Better Tennis by Harry Hopman (Kaye & Ward. 1972). £1.10.
Improving Your Tennis by C. M. Jones (Faber & Faber. 1973). £1.75.
A Tennis Professional's Notebook by Dudley Georgeson, L.T.A. Registered coach. (Obtainable from: 54 Lyndhurst Gardens, Finchley, London, N.3). 20p post paid.

Part Three
Skills, Practices and Fitness

Practice sessions should be performed with as much determination and firmness as for an actual match – and the ball needs to be hit harder; but not just belted wildly so as to destroy the essential sense of timing and touch.

Fitness is not some extraneous substance to be inserted into tennis like a prescription, but a continuous process of high quality living. While everyone doesn't possess it, tennis players can't afford to be without it, if they have ambitions of becoming impressive performers. Then fitness and tennis are a perfect match.

19

Check List of Teaching and Training Points (for teachers and pupils alike)

Teaching pupils in school

* Interest and keenness is sustained by the teacher handling his class and the subject in a lively and stimulating manner (basic to any subject).

* Early teaching and coaching best done by the class method; but plan subsequent lessons to make a balance between *class*, *small group* (twos, threes, fours – plus) and *individual* coaching.

* Regarding interest and enthusiasm: it pays dividends to let pupils 'have a go' as soon as possible after introducing a new skill. They quickly gain a limited experience and are more ready for additional guidance towards improvement.

* Relate practices to a competitive situation, particularly with small group work. This keeps their interest honed to a sharp edge.

* Fun at an early age is essential for sustained interest. Group lessons can give the most pleasure.

* The emerging pupils with ability and promise are then coached individually during and outside of P.E. classes, after two or three years of group training.

* Improvement through pleasure requires the provision of incentives and targets, geared to the group's capacity. Competition is important and necessary.

* Success in turn further stimulates interest and morale.

Tennis for Schools

* Points for praise and encouragement must be found even if a pupil is defeated in play. Something good can be found to say about everyone.

* Emerging champions of rare ability demonstrate a thoroughness born of a tremendous attention to detail and willingness to train.

* Emphasise to pupils the three main factors for improving ability: (1) attention to minute detail;
    (2) applied concentration;
    (3) personal pleasure and delight in practising and playing tennis.

* Impress upon pupils the need to dominate the ball, not be dominated by its velocity, flight and bounce. They must feel to be in charge of their game.

* Pupils need to be made aware of and to experience the additional touch shots; but just when they will start to include them in their personal repertoire is largely their concern.

* *Fundamental principles:* during a period of highly individual, spectacular styles, the 'classic style' still exists; but deviations are certainly permissible to suit individual characteristics. Certain basic *fundamentals* however, are unwavering in their importance:
    (1) Balance and steadiness of mind;
    (2) footwork and stance;
    (3) control of racket;
    (4) swing (backswing, stroke, follow-through);
    (5) watching the ball and anticipating play.

A perfect blend of these gives that smooth fluency which creates a deceptive impression of simplicity and ease – a characteristic of all top athletes and sportsmen.

* *Instructional sequence:* a shorthand reminder of a practical teaching programme.
    (1) Shadowing (class copying coach's demo.)
    (2) Stroke practice with dropped ball (groups)
    (3) Partner 'feeding' balls for stroke practice
    (4) Practice in rallying (pairs)
    (5) Stroke play in game situation
    (6) Grooving the stroke (at every opportunity)

Check List of Teaching and Training Points

Pointers for pupils

* Learn and gain inspiration from watching the stars of tennis, but don't try to imitate their style of play blindly; rather, try to figure out *why* they play the way they do. Then see how you match up with this.

* If you are left-handed, be pleased. It is an advantage to be a lefty in tennis. It certainly adds to your opponent's problems on court. Their interpretation of your game has to be reversed, continuously, adding to their labours.

* Weigh-up in your mind which of these two types of game may suit your personality and requirements:
    (1) aggressive, hard-hitting, serve-and-volley, with a compulsive urge to win quickly, decisively; or
    (2) friendly, easy-going fun-game; content *just to keep the ball in play and simply happy to enjoy yourself without much* aggression?

Even if you go for (2), you must still play with some tigerish aggressiveness; remember, your opponent needs to be extended to enjoy his game.

* The forehand and backhand groundstrokes are the backbone of a good tennis game, so master these before playing around with other, maybe more spectacular shots. And learn them thoroughly together, so you do not have to favour your forehand through lack of backhand confidence. *Never run around either shot.*

* Big game built on *Steadiness, Control, Stroking.*

* *Grips:* learn the three basic grips thoroughly until they feel completely natural. These are the 'Shake-hands' forehand grip, the 'Backhand' grip, and the service or 'Chopper' grip. Other two recognised grips, the Western and Continental are seldom used by good players, so why confuse the issue? Ignore them. However, your own personal variation of the basic grips is allowable and entirely dependent on how comfortable and natural they feel. It's up to you. But seek early advice.

    When you take up your grip, spread your fingers to get maximum *feel* of the handle, and use your thumb for maximum support, and strength (especially in the backhand stroke), grasping as near to the butt as feels comfortable for the most length, swing and power.

* The first rule of any shot: *watch the flight of the ball* from your opponent's racket right to the point of impact with your own strings.

* Train to *move forward* towards the oncoming ball in an attacking manner. This means reading the play in advance of each shot. Discipline yourself not to retreat backwards except in dire emergencies (generally because you've been caught napping).

* Position yourself to hit the ball at the peak of its bounce (not on the rise), as if it were teed-up and *waist high* for maxim control and power. This means you'll have to train to bend your knees a lot. Don't be lazy and think that scooping-up shots without getting down to them is good enough. Girls are often guilty here. Modern tennis is for tough, energetic athletes, but it doesn't decrease a girl's feminity. So don't worry on that score, ladies!

* Don't crowd the ball with your strokes. Get maximum length from racket plus arm for greater power, as if it were a natural seeming extension of your arm.

* Learn to capture the feel of racket-ball contact. Think about making a *long contact* between ball and strings. Think of the ball actually making a split-second 'pocket' in the centre of the racket face. This gives more ball control.

* Place your returns where you decide are to your advantage, not where the flight of the ball suggests. You lead not follow!

* Place the ball where your opponent is *not*.

* Cover the court by intelligent anticipation and keep in a dominant central position.

* Keep moving – don't be caught flat-footed and off balance.

Other points for anyone who cares to use them:

* Avoid taking the ball off the back foot under pressure. This is defensive play. Practise attacking play off the front foot.

Check List of Teaching and Training Points

This requires extra alertness and the ability to read the play in advance of your own shots (and I've said this plenty of times).

* Training demands total involvement and concentration. This may be more tiring, but far-and-away more valuable than aimless 'knocking-up' and 'friendly' set-playing. No doubt you'll tell me to let you decide just what you are out there with a racket for!

* Mental imagery and nerve transmission are inter-related and must be used to *groove the stroke*. Think into the movement!

* Pre-season learning and training: 'You learn to ski in the summer and play golf in the winter.' (William James, American psychologist) You can play tennis all the year round.

* Lastly, consider *Power* versus *Touch* and weigh-up how to get the best out of both in your game. Don't try to kill every shot – control before power.

Practice

* Every practice must be treated seriously, with the concentration and determination of an important match.
* Total concentration is as vital in practice as in competition.
* Practice with a purpose by setting yourself a target.
* Use the practice session to apply all the coaching points you can remember – unless you feel that you are bogging down your pupils under too much technicality unrelieved by essential fun.
* A practice session should be for self-improvement, not just to pass the time away.
* End your practice session with a feeling of achievement and fulfilment.
* Before leaving the court, start thinking about and planning the next practice session.
* Make a note of your weakness as your main target for next time.

Tennis for Schools

* 'Practice in your head' as much as you can, wherever you are.

* Practice 'ghost strokes' or shadowing in private, with or without your racket.

20
Sample Lesson Plan

Instructional lessons should be – *Objective/Creative/Imaginative/ Informative/Competitive* and *Progressive* and have – *Variety/ Challenge* and *Continuity* and stimulate – *Interest/Enjoyment/ Self-improvement/Self-discipline/Sportsmanship/Fitness* and *Fulfilment*. Which is another way of saying that 'off-the-cuff', mock-up non-lessons don't pay-off in the long run.

An organised lesson plan provides the framework from which to introduce and teach the skills and practices and to convey a real sense of progress.

Changing, equipment, free practice

* Pupils are encouraged to change quickly, collect tennis equipment individually and start practising without delay. This will be in pairs on what they previously learnt.
    (a) Training in self-discipline and responsible behaviour obviously will be necessary.
    (b) The idea of 'Free Practice' should provide an incentive for them to get out and practising without messing about.
    (c) They will benefit from a changing room briefing on any specific point.

Re-assembly

* A speedy class assembly for lesson organisation and commencement of official instruction under direct teacher-coach guidance.

Warm-up

* Limbering-up total body structure, both with or without rackets.

Tennis for Schools

Instruction

* Re-assembly and class positioning for:
  (a) Demonstration – explanation – shadowing (class).
  (b) Shadowing with teacher and partner checking (pairs).

Class and group practising

* Teacher freely – moving, checking – coaching – correcting – encouraging.
  (a) *Class* arranged into 'Feeders' and 'Strikers', either across court with backs to side-netting; or on opposite sides of the centre net; or utilising spare field or playground space.
  (b) *Small groups* (twos, three, fours – plus) practising specific assignments according to space.
  (c) *Tennis activities* for fun, fitness, technical instruction, competitive practice – for variety and to sustain interest and keenness.

Fitness training

* Strength and endurance exercise, both *class* and *partner* activity, as straight training and game-like activity.

    Make it clear to the pupils why they are being asked (compelled?) to perform such 'strenuous' activity. Pupil co-operation is essential.

Game

* Dual-purpose activity:
  (a) Putting into realistic practice what they've learnt.
  (b) Their 'reward' for behaving and co-operating in the total lesson (this should be made clear).
  (c) Introduces the essential competitive element to maintain interest and enthusiasm.

Time: 40 minutes minimum. 45 to 60 minutes preferable (ideally, this is actual lesson-time).

Sample Lesson Plan

NOTES
1. This is biased towards a direct tennis lesson and not representative of a general P.E. class as such. Swinging all the instruction and training over to one sport this way, may not be the entire reason for having a group of pupils report for P.E. and Games. Teachers are usually careful to avoid one activity from 'taking over the lesson'.
2. On the other hand, you may decide to keep the lesson purely a tennis coaching one and leave the fitness training for another type of P.E. lesson. It could depend upon how you read your lesson and see your tennis image; or whether or not you are a P.E. teacher or a tennis coach. They're not necessarily synonymous.
3. Lesson construction is a varied, even a controversial and provocative subject – and why not? The idea is to stimulate thought and move on to action. A big asset is to be flexible, even unpredictable; but never plod, plod, plod.
4. Another point about this fitness training. If you don't make room for it in the tennis lesson, where do you imagine it will be done? If you are the tennis coach, do you just leave items like fitness exercise to the P.E. department, assuming they are taking care of it during the week somehow? Do you just interpret your role as responsible for strokes, tactics and technique? Is this unfair? Yet, simply giving pupils a racket and a couple of balls each and asking them to shadow you and to build up their stroke-bank, is hardly developing their total physical mechanism in a balanced way, in fact, it's breeding one-sided development. This is a common failing or hazard of many sports. How, for example, does the cardiovascular system get the rigorous stimulation and exercise it needs, especially for endurance fitness? And what about the muscle-groups on the non-racket-arm side? If you are of the P.E. staff, then you'll have these considerations in the forefront of your mind and be figuring-out just how they should be fitted into your term's work.

SPECIAL POINTS

1. Quick-change at beginning of class period, to get out of the rooms, collect equipment and make a start on 'Free Practice' without delay, either individually or with partner.

Tennis for Schools

2. This is a chance for pupils to recap what was taught in last lesson.

3. Quiet, rapid response to teacher's call for organisational and instructional assemblies is essential – one would have thought obvious. Getting the class to understand and co-operate with this first principle of teaching may be difficult in some cases; nevertheless, pupils must be persuaded to respond according to decent social behaviour and to see the reason for it – despite the pretended misunderstanding of a few militants. It's for everyone's benefit to capture their attention when you have some important teaching point to convey. Although who's fault is it when the class won't attend because they're bored with the teacher?

4. *Time limits for practices:* are influenced by whether or not the period is P.E. or games. Short sessions are necessary to fit into an overcrowded P.E. lesson; but a more generous allocation is permissible for a flexible games period.

Sample Lesson Plan

Another form of lesson plan

A OPENING ACTIVITY/WARM-UP (reduce time-lag)
B SKILL-TRAINING/CLASS SHADOWING (without balls)
C INDIVIDUAL/PARTNER PRACTICE/COACHING (non-competitive)
D PARTNER/SMALL GROUP ACTIVITIES/PRACTICES (competitive)
E GAMES/SETS/MATCHES

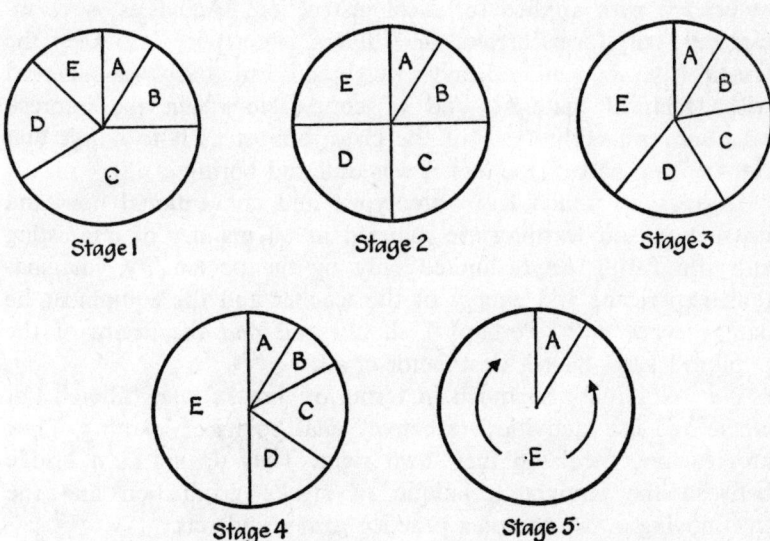

'A' section remains constant to encourage quick changing and early start.
Competitive games and sets gradually take-over as skills and ability increases.

Proportional allocation of other sections depend upon general progress of class. Individuals can always be permitted more flexibility and freedom for progress.

Occasionally permit total lesson for games, sets, matches.

21
Activities and Skills

There might have been a time once when skills were strictly associated with applied technical instruction. 'Activities' were incidental, play-form 'breaks' and 'fillers', interspersed to keep the lesson from becoming heavy, weighted-down and over-balanced with technical material – and of course, to retain the interest, attention and enthusiasm of the class; almost as if to admit that the teaching part of the lesson was dull and boring.

Lessons are much less stereotyped and conventional now and instruction and learning are married in all manner of interesting and stimulating ways, limited only by the personality, imagination, experience and energy of the teacher and the equipment he has to work with. Perhaps I should add *and* the desire of the pupil to learn – the trickiest factor of all.

We don't think so much in terms of 'breaks' and 'fillers', but create and use 'activities' to convey vital points of learning. They are teaching media in their own right. They do act as a bridge between the straight technique of stroke production and the free-moving, more complex practice games and sets.

Avoid: a lesson-form of purely technical instruction, playing games and sets. It can be boring and fail to stretch and extend the pupil, or to note and correct weaknesses. Weaker, less accomplished performers are particularly at a disadvantage, to them, straight tennis can be most frustrating and discouraging, because technically it can be a difficult game and many aren't willing to scramble.

Promote: a learning sequence based on the following lesson content.

Instruction

(a) *Stroke production,* basic (planned technical instruction, preferably brief and pointed in easily digestible amounts).

Activities and Skills

(b) *Stroke use* (what best to do with your newly-acquired skills).

(c) *Tactics* (how to use the court, anticipate your opponent's play, positioning and placing).

(d) *Rules* (bring in rules as a natural part and sequence of the particular instruction of (a), (b) and (c) progressively).

Activities

(a) *Class/group* (an average P.E. class of 30-plus may have to be kept interested and exercised. This means at least three groups of 10 on a change-over basis).

(b) *Small group work* (threes and fours-plus, sharing duties and practices: feeding, striking, collecting. Including target practice).

(c) *Partner work* (based on 'feeders' and 'strikers'; competitive where suitable).

(d) *Individual practice* (stroke production, rallying, target practice using side netting, 'Dan Maskell Tennis Trainer' (wall-net), a tennis wall, or improvising any available and permissible wall space).

Practice games

(a) *All courts* in use for singles or doubles, or adaptations.

(b) *Improvised areas* (rope between other games posts; from centre posts to side netting if sufficient space; playground and playingfield space; use chairs, string and benches to substitue for centre netting).

(c) *Court use plus practice groups* (organise on a change-over basis so use is fair throughout).

(d) *Scoring, rules, etiquette* (this will be introduced naturally to both class and individual players as the teacher judges the need and the demand emerges – in small amounts).

Special points

1. Introduce competitive activity in all four sections of the ACTIVITIES; but make the scoring and competition realistic in keeping with performer's age and ability.
2. All practices and activities should be as interesting and enjoyable as if they were playing an actual game.
3. Select the activity to be used according to the kind of skill to be practised: e.g. groundstrokes, volleying, lob; or for improvement of a quality like accuracy. Every activity has its personal characteristic requiring a particular skill with the racket.
4. Waiting for a turn may be unavoidable; but the time needn't be wasted: (1) act as umpire and score-keeper; (2) keep a supply of balls available for the 'feeders' and 'strikers', (3) there is learning in watching – act as deputy coach.
5. Space is always at a premium with tennis classes, so maximum use has to be made, particularly by way of small group activities and practices rotated as a training circuit.
6. Activities should help the teacher to avoid overdoing static practices and risking the boredom of his class. Get the groups or pairs off to practise their assignments with the minimum delay. The chief aim is *'Have a go!'*

22
Shadowing and Feeding

These two form a natural sequence in teaching and, as I've mentioned them a few times, they deserve a recognised place. In Chapter 9 on 'Groundstrokes', I introduced shadowing as a form of Pupil Practice. Here is some more help along those lines.

Shadowing

* Have a racket in your hand and go through the motions with every new grip and stroke. Do this while sorting out the movement in your mind and not rely on memory.
* Practise all foot work, stance and strokes with a racket in your hand, starting from the essential 'Predator' Stance or ready position. The performer has to get his body conditioned to responding fast with the impediment of a racket attached to one arm.
* Indoor shadowing is valuable, so do it whenever you can, having checked first that you won't sweep the priceless ornament off the TV, or bash father's 'funny-bone'.
* This is *grooving the stroke* and *building a mental stroke bank*. It can be done without a racket when you're hard-pushed – like waiting at the dentist's, or doing playground duty. Only try not to use too obvious facial and limb movements when grooving in public, or you'll get some funny looks. I mean, how are other people to know what's on your mind?
* When doing shadowing in class practice, make sure there is enough space all round to swing a racket safely. The teacher checks this from time to time.
* Left-handed players should be positioned to avoid clashing rackets with right-handed neighbours. Their position must

Tennis for Schools

also be considered in relationship with the teacher's demonstrations.

* The teacher has to change position frequently, according to the different strokes, so all advantage points can be seen by the maximum number of pupils.
* The class should all be on the same side of the court, facing the net and the teacher. As he demonstrates and explains, they can be shadowing his every move, getting the feel of the new stroke in their bodies.
* These may be semi-static practices, but to off-set boredom they must be short, sharp and dynamic – the instructor can be any size so long as he's a live wire!
* His voice has to be heard without strain also by the pupils furthest away. Can he check now and then to make sure distant pupils are not straining to hear?
* Encourage pupils into the shadowing habit while they're watching and actively following instructions and demonstrations, and both with and without a racket in all manner of other situations, the idea is not to waste a valuable moment in the grooving business – but be considerate of the House Master!
* Make use of the pupils who are grasping the strokes well to demonstrate alongside the teacher, or in front of the class while the teacher moves about freely checking and helping.

Feeding

This is a most important skill for the teacher, tennis coach and even the pupil's partner to have. The learner depends upon skilful feeding for his progress, his whole training and practice is intimately wrapped up with it – but only if it is accurate. Sloppy, inaccurate feeding is not only a waste of time, it delays the learning process and encourages bad stroke production. A pretty obvious comment I suppose. Anyway, it's up to the teacher-coach to add this skill to his teaching repertoire and to make sure that pupils learn how to do it and use it as well. In fact, it's all part of the tennis game.

Shadowing and Feeding

TWO KINDS OF FEEDING:

(1) teacher-coach, or another player sends (feeds) balls to the striker according to the type of stroke being practised.

(2) striker-player-pupil feeds balls to himself so he can hit them for individual practice.

DIFFERENT METHODS OF FEEDING

* Feeder stands close-by and drops the ball for the striker.

* Feeder, from further away, throws the balls *underhand*, with agreed pauses for the striker to regain the ready position and to receive instruction and advice.

* Feeder delivers a *series* of balls underhand – a progression of the previous method. This is to imitate a rally in a game, with timed intervals between balls at a realistic tempo (which can be varied to simulate game conditions).

* Feeder now *uses his racket* from the other side of the net, to develop the timed series method of delivery, producing faster balls more realistically.

* Feeder now *rallies* with the striker, using rackets. This requires skill in tempo, consistency and ability to direct and place the ball for the striker's benefit, giving him experience at all kinds of shots.

* Feeder and striker play games or a set. But throughout this competitive session, the teacher uses opportunities and breaks to convey information, advice and general coaching, as well as trying to feed the ball into predetermined areas of the court using a broad variety of shots to provide wide stroke experience in the striker.

NOTE: where the feeder can honestly admit he hasn't the skill with his racket to feed series and rallies accurately, then the next best method to give the striker the experience he needs is accurate *underhand* feeding. It is important to realise this alternative. Never be too proud to admit this racket weakness and make it good by hand feeding.

Tennis for Schools

Feeding techniques

1. GROUNDSTROKE PRACTICE:

(a) Striker turns sideways, ball dropped a comfortable distance from his leading foot.

(b) Striker starts from ready position and must *turn* and *step in* to play the shot (feeder adjusts delivery).

(c) Feeder develops this by dropping ball sufficient distance from striker to make him *move towards it* to produce his stroke.

(d) Take this further by feeding balls at varying distances and positions from striker, so he has to move *sideways, forwards* or *backwards* to stroke properly.

(e) Feeder now drops or tosses balls from greater height to give striker more time to contact ball at its *most efficient height for impact* (just after peak of rise).

(f) Allow more time for this judgement on the backhand side (it takes striker fractionally longer to prepare).

(g) Feed with change of *pace, direction, length* and *height,* to quicken striker's reactions.

(h) Do racket feeding to produce consistent forehand-backhand rallying (or continue with hand feeding for greater accuracy, having a fair supply of balls at your feet and in the left hand).

2. SMASH PRACTICE:

(a) Feeder throws up the ball from a position just in front of and to one side of the striker.

(b) Increase height and variety of throw as striker improves.

(c) Feed from the other end of the court with high deliveries.

3. VOLLEYING:

(a) High volley – deliver ball to arrive at shoulder height or above, on striker's racket side.

Shadowing and Feeding

(b) Low volley – deliver to arrive at knee height (or between ankle and waist).

(c) Racket feeding using volleys to reduce time-lag and distance between feeder and striker.

NOTES:
1. The teacher should practise to become proficient at all methods of feeding to produce balls against which the pupils can gain experience with all the basic strokes.
2. After the dropping of the balls stage has been passed, feeding from near the net on the opposite side for greater accuracy is best.
3. Feeder should increase the sequence of balls fed by hand to simulate various types of rallies for the striker's benefit.
4. Accurate feeding increases a pupil's confidence by giving evenly-timed, consistent practice.

Wall feeding

This is an invaluable practice for the single pupil, or together with a partner. I have even had four keen boys working together on one small wall area, feeding the ball and keeping it on the rally by the rotational method: (1) feeds, steps aside for (2) to take his place and feed on the rebound for (3), and so on ... In fact, they became addicted to the practice.

If it is a permanent tennis wall (home-made or otherwise), it will be marked-up with a 3 ft. net line and also targets. Also, have three *restriction lines* drawn on the ground at distances of 10, 15 and 20 feet parallel to the base of the wall (The 10 ft. line will be sufficient challenge for beginners – obviously they are not supposed to cross it).

Both indoors and outdoors, a wall can usually be found to include in group practices, or to provide the individual or the couple something useful and enjoyable to do while waiting for their turn on court. A wall is undoubtedly part of tennis training. I wouldn't like to be without it.

Dan Maskell Tennis Trainer (*wall-net*)

It is always handy to have a portable trainer for stroke production and this particular free-standing wall-net is especially useful

Tennis for Schools

both indoors and outdoors. It is to tennis what the cradle is to cricket, possibly more so, and can accommodate four performers together, at a pinch; two can get more valuable practice, of course, while the individual can enjoy hours of concentrated stroke work. The point is, this kind of portable equipment can be available whenever anyone feels like brushing-up their groundstrokes, volleys and service – grooving them from continuous feeding. It is constructed of light-weight tubular metal stainless steel springs and nylon mesh and manufactured by Latika (Sports Equipment) Ltd., 430 Bath Road, Slough, Bucks, England.

23

Selected Tennis Activities

These give enjoyable, concentrating practice for individuals, pairs and small groups, for development of ball sense, racket control, tactics and court use. They help especially in developing *Stroke Use* in a competitive situation, on the understanding that the basic spade work of *Stroke Production* has been previously introduced and is well on its way. Then, an acceptable balance between stroke practices and game-like activities should be achieved.

Ball sense training

Get pupils (classes) on to ball sense exercises and activities early before the tennis season. Pre-season preparation doesn't have to have a court, or even a partner. Think of any spare time and space as valuable for improving tennis.

WHAT IS BALL SENSE?

'Ball sense' is understanding of what is happening to the ball when hit, in flight, or bouncing and how best to react to it.

(a) How hard was it hit?

(b) Was topspin, backspin or slice applied?

(c) What is its speed in flight?

(d) How high will it be through the air?

(e) Is it rising or falling?

(f) Where will it cross the net?

(g) How high will it bounce and which direction?

Tennis for Schools

(h) Will its spin affect its bounce and where?

(i) How should I best position myself to hit it?

(j) Should I take it on my strongest side?

(k) I should judge to hit it at the peak of its rise.

(l) I must feel long contact with ball and strings.

Practice at these activities will sharpen judgement, improve anticipation, quicken reaction time, develop handling ability, ball control and instinctive and accurate use of the racket.

Ball Handling Without Racket: throwing – bouncing – catching

1. Throw and catch with a partner, or in group, varying the distance, height, speed and direction of throwing to make the catcher work hard in moving about.
2. Throw and bounce ball to partner, with variations like the previous. Make different types of bounces. Progress from two-handed catching to one-handed, then single hand alternatively.
3. Throw and bounce two ball simultaneously with partner, synchronising the throwing to each other by calling 'Now!'
4. Throwing and aiming to hit targets placed on ground between partners, such as a ball box, shuttlecock container, skittle, hoop, and objects getting smaller. Agree on a scoring system for hitting and catching (lose points for dropped catches).
5. Develop throwing and spinning the ball, anticipating the direction of the bounce after the spin and moving to meet it.
6. Throw the ball higher than your head to comfortable service height, then try to keep it in the air by punching upwards. Keep a casual score.
7. Reaction catching in pairs: catcher has his back turned at moment of throw, but at pre-arranged signal from partner he turns to make the catch before being bypassed by the ball.
8. Service throw-up (individually): from the service stance practise action of both arms, but stop the racket in the backscratch position and continue placing up the ball. Let it fall and be checked for accuracy into a small hoop or box placed about a foot in front of and just to the right of your leading foot.

Selected Tennis Activities

9. Play 'Piggy-in-the-Middle' for a bit of fun and to quicken the senses: either in circle formation or with just three. The 'Piggy' has to intercept the ball which is thrown briskly backwards and forwards among the outside players. Last player to throw the ball before interception becomes 'Piggy' and changes places in the middle.

10. TENNIS WITHOUT RACKETS. Keep to identical tennis rules, but throw the ball instead of using rackets. *Serve:* overarm throw; but with all other shots, throwing hand must not be raised above shoulder level without releasing the ball. Rallies are maintained by catching the ball on the fly or after one bounce and it must be thrown back without delay. Catch with either hand; but if one-handed the ball must be returned from the catching hand, left or right.

NOTE: there are scores of activities to be adapted from P.E. and games books all over the country. I'll be listing some.

Groundstrokes and drives

CONSISTENCY RALLIES: start from readiness behind centre of baseline. Begin with forehand and *keep it going*, counting the strokes. Only count shots that land in singles court between service and baselines. The rally ends if the ball is hit out, short or into the net. Switch over to practise backhand. Soon as you feel ready, hit series of alternate forehand-backhand shots, returning to central readiness position between each one.

ACCURACY RALLIES: 'Keep the ball alive' with a partner, anywhere in court at first with forehand-backhand shots. Introduce accuracy by *rallying up and down the tram-lines*. Increase the concentration and aim by placing targets on court to be hit (skittles, ball boxes, small hoops). Have points scoring for rewarding hits.

RUNNING ROUND GAME: line of pupils (12 maximum) at one end of court, facing coach who has a supply of balls ready to feed at the net. Each pupil moves on to court, receives his allotted ball in turn from the coach, plays his shot, runs on round the court past the coach and so on back to the end of his line. It is most helpful if he acts as ballboy during the circuit. Any stroke except the service can be practised.

Tennis for Schools

RUNNING ROUND RALLY: 10 to 16 players each with racket and ball, disperse around the court's perimeter and into a steady trot round. After the initial two circuits, each player hits a medium-paced shot down court as he passes the centre of a baseline. The player nearest the opposite baseline returns the shot at medium-pace down centre-court to the next player at the end from where the rally started and so on... Each player should get two strokes, one from each end of the court during every circuit. If a shot is mishit, or a ball hit out, the player responsible keeps the rally going by introducing the ball from his hand.

RUNNING ROUND FOR POINTS: 12 players per court are a preferable maximum. No one drops out in this game. Players trot round the outer edge, coach names a stroke and each pupil in turn uses it to hit into the singles court – on the run. Points given for successful hits. Target boxes can be placed 6 ft. inside the baseline for training greater accuracy.

PRESSURE TRAINING: for three or four players. Two at the net feeding the third who operates from the baseline, going for everything they send down (direct, wide, long, short, fast – aiming to fully stretch the baseline striker). The fourth player acts as ballboy to keep the feeders supplied without a break. All positions interchange frequently.

Service, lob and smash

OVERARM THROWING CONTEST: as this is the action used in serving, plenty of practice is called for. Throwing can be for distance, height, or at targets. Actual serving with a racket should be practised after this contest to relate the action of throwing to the function of serving.

TEAM SERVICE CONTEST: pick up teams, maximum six-a-side (12 to a court). Distribute all available balls equally among one team's members at one end of the court. This team spreads out behind their baseline and starts serving together down court until their supply of balls are used up. The other team collect the balls. The coach stands by the service court to count out loud the number of balls to be served fairly into that area.

For the second half, the other team collects the same number of balls, then try to beat the first team's score.

TARGET SERVING: two teams of six serving from the right and

Selected Tennis Activities

left courts of the same baseline, at targets placed in the opposite service squares (large, empty tins make a pleasing noise when hit). Each player serves his first and second service *twice*, scoring a point for hitting the target. Move both teams and targets to cover both important corners of the service squares from time-to-time. Non-servers act as ball-boys.

TARGET BASHING: six to twelve empty ball boxes are spaced across the service courts about a foot from the service line. One team starts with all the balls distributed equally, spreads out behind the opposite baseline and begins serving together at the targets on the other side of the net. Aim: to clear the maximum number of boxes from the court by hitting them with the service shots, in a *limited time of 4 minutes*. Each team tries for a better score.

POINTING THE SMASH: individual practice to improve judgement, aim, balance and stance. Point with the free left hand to the falling ball as you get set to smash it. Train yourself in this technique by tossing ball after ball into the air, pointing and smashing.

LOB AND SMASH IN TWOS OR THREES:

(a) one player lobs 10 times, the other smashes, then change.
(b) Keep a lob-smash rally going, but try to win.
(c) Play a threesome, with the ends lobbing over the middle who tries to smash. Change places.

THE SMASH: the feeder stands behind one baseline centre with a good supply of balls. The rest of the group go behind the opposite baseline. They take it in turns to move up court to just inside the service line. There they smash three lobs from the feeder, then collect the three balls, return them to the feeder and rejoin the group, while another player moves up to receive lobs. After the feeder has given each player his ration of three lobs, he changes places with one of them.

LOB AND SMASH IN FOURS: two sets of four players to each court, keeping to a half each. Each team places one player for smashing nearer to the net, two players facing each other down-court from opposite baselines and directly in line with the smasher,

155

Tennis for Schools

while the fourth player is freely mobile, acting as ball-boy. Number 3 starts with a lob to the first one, who smashes and between them they try to keep a *lob-smash-lob* rally going. In a breakdown, another ball is lobbed for continuity. If a lob clears the smasher, he lets the player behind take it to hit a groundstroke back to the original lobber, who lobs again towards the net smasher and more rallies. Players interchange roles after an agreed time, or a number of attempted smashes.

Volleying

GOALKEEPING VOLLEYS: chalk goals on a wall, indicating net height. The shooter uses groundstrokes (single shots or rallies), the goalkeeper uses volleys only to defend and reject. An agreed shooting line must be marked in keeping with the strength and ability of the players, and to give the keeper a reasonable chance. The wall or netting at his rear will deter him from swinging at the volleys and constantly remind him to punch or block instead.

ATTACKING VOLLEYS: each player collects three balls and stands spaced behind the baseline, faced by his partner at the other end of the court in similar circumstances. A plays a ground-stroke to partner B, then moves in towards the net. B returns it and also moves towards the net. A now volleys or half-volleys, then B does the same and they both continue to move in on each other using short, sharp volleys. The last exchanges will be machine gun volleys between partners close to the net. The player who mishits has to introduce another ball to keep the rally going. The first to use up his three balls loses that round. Service can be used instead of groundstrokes to start the rally.

PATTERN VOLLEYING: with four to a group, each court can take 24. Doubles formation facing across a net, or improvised net: players 1 and 2 facing 3 and 4 at a distance suitable to their ability. Player 1 volleys across to 3, who does the same *at an angle* to 2, who volleys straight to 4, who *angle volleys* back to 1 and so on. Count out loud the number of consecutive shots played without the ball bouncing. Neighbouring groups will be encouraged to compete. Change the pattern and the players' positions to vary the experience. A new ball is introduced by any player who mishits and upsets the sequence.

Selected Tennis Activities

CIRCLE VOLLEY: about 12 players spread out into a circle covering half a doubles court, with no one less than 3 ft. from the net or an outer line. A player volleys the ball across the ring to anyone who is handy to receive it. Volleying continues this way with the whole team trying not to let the ball touch the floor. The number of strokes played before a breakdown should be counted to introduce the competitive spirit (team against team; or team trying to beat its own score). The only rule is: receiver of a shot *must not hit it straight back* to the previous striker.

VOLLEY PUNCHING IN PAIRS: work with a partner, striker has his back against the stop netting, the feeder about 10 paces away. Feed a ball underhand to striker's forehand, shoulder high; striker volleys it back for the feeder to catch. This catching improves the feeder's reaction and keeps the practice going. When the forehand has been mastered, change to backhand volleying. After that do alternate forehand-backhand volleys, remembering to change the grip. *No backswing* – the stop netting will deter that.

Wall practices

A wall is valuable for the individual who needs practice but hasn't got a partner. It's good for couples and small groups too. With careful choice, most walls will provide faithful service, but be considerate of other people's property. A permanent practice wall for the school is best, because it's designed for the job and can have targets, goals and a net line painted on it.

WALL TARGET 'BREAK': using your regular practice wall with its permanent painted target. You need the top half of a circle with a diameter of 6 ft., painted parallel with the net line and 12 in. above it. This is divided into four sections: three outer radii at 36 in., 26 in. and 16 in., and a centre bull with a radius of 6 in. painted-in solid. These give scores of 5, 3, 2, 1, points. A 'Break' is achieved by a player rallying against the target, adding each hit according to its place on the marked half-circle or bull, before a mishit or wildly-hit shot ends that particular break. For example: four bulls consecutively, plus one hit on the outer ring, followed by a mishit, gives a total score of 21 for that 'Break' (A line hit counts the higher score). Records of the target's use can be kept up to date and published on a nearby noticeboard,

Tennis for Schools

for various age groups. This would attract interest and provide strong incentive.

WALL RALLIES: for the person on his own and a wall that can have goals marked (chalked) on it, say 12 ft. wide (or smaller for experienced players). The player feeds himself by dropping and bouncing the ball, then starts the rally with a choosen stroke, trying to keep the shots hitting inside the goal area. Forehands, backhands, volleys, half-volleys or combinations of strokes can be named and used. The practice is competitive by counting the rallies and trying to beat one's own score, or that of a neighbouring player.

GROUP RALLIES: same idea as above, but played by a small group or team. The group splits into two lines, on the left and right of the goal and behind a *restriction line* drawn on the ground parallel to the wall and about 20 ft. away. This is to discourage over-hitting and make the practice fairer. Shots which rebound beyond the line are counted 'out'. Players take it in turns to hit medium pace balls into the goal, using forehand from the left, backhand from the right and moving across to take a new position behind their opposite line after playing the shot. This way they should keep the forehand-backhand rally going.

WALL VOLLEYS: a line of individuals along the wall can get this practice in comfortably (allowing for safety spacing). The player feeds himself then starts with a groundstroke, followed by a volley and tries to keep the rally going with a succession of volleys. He can remember his score for competition with his neighbours.

3-WAY VOLLEYS: the player now tries volleying from *three different distances* for different results. (1) 20 ft. for low volleys (2) 15 ft. for medium to high volleys (3) 10 ft. for fast-reaction volleys, or even as close as 5 ft. to speed-up reflexes still more. It is an idea to chalk the appropriate restriction lines on the ground; or use court marking paint.

SERVE AND VOLLEY: a form of pressure training for individuals, or small groups, as there isn't a lot of time to play the volley. The group lines-up behind the restriction line of 15–20 ft. The first player serves, moves in to volley the rebound and continues volleying until a breakdown. He then moves to the end of the line and the next player takes over. Try to serve to strike the wall about 5 ft. (or about 2 ft. above the net line). This is where it is most useful to have permanent targets painted.

Selected Tennis Activities

HALF-VOLLEYS: a wall gives the best practice for half-volleys. Starting with groundstrokes, goood anticipation and quick forward and backward movements will turn a good proportion of these into half-volleys. The coach should always remind his pupils that this is purely an emergency stroke, played to get out of trouble when the opponent has given no alternative.

Half-volleys require the player to bend his knees and get down to the shot.

THE TREADMILL: an unrelenting forward and backward movement for improving fitness and ball control. The individual player hits his first groundstroke from the restriction line, moves in fast to volley the rebound, moves back in time to groundstroke the return, in again fast to volley and so on, in and out with speed, *trying not to break the sequence.* Aim for a 20-shot rally to get the full flavor and meaning of 'The Treadmill'.

TENNIS SQUASH: a fast game for two, or four if space permits. A suitable goal is required on the wall and a restriction line at 10 or 15 ft. on the ground. Underhand serve to start the rally, then any type of shot may be used. Tennis or tabletennis scoring can be used for competition.

The foregoing are just a small selection of a great variety of activities to be obtained from certain books or booklets, some of which I've listed at the end of Part Three.

Padder-tennis

This is a most popular and useful game in its own right, as well as being a valuable lead-in game for tennis itself. Its stroke play is practically identical and its scoring is the same. Having a smaller court, it makes more economical use of existing space; more courts can be chalked or painted in an available area (it is an excellent playground game). So let's get down to it.

Padder-tennis posts and bases: tubular steel uprights, fitted to solid cast weight bases with carrying handles, guaranteed indestructible (manufacturer's blurb).

Padder-tennis nets: nylon mesh with headline and headband. Both from: Triangle Sports Equipment, 6 Tudor Road, Hackney, London E.9.

Padder-tennis bats: there are two on the market, one is similar

Tennis for Schools

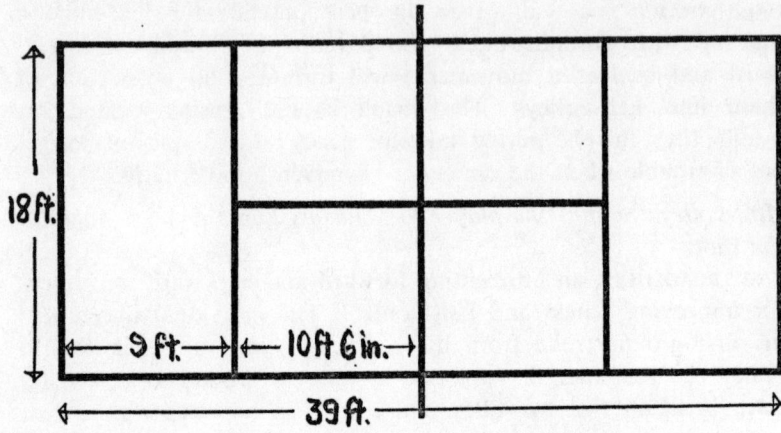

Fig. 44. Padder-tennis (Alternative size 36 ft. x 18 ft.) Net height: 2 ft. 6 in. at post, 2 ft. 3 in. at centre

to a largish table-tennis bat, which I don't recommend. The other is a little larger, more attractively designed in varnished hardwood, by Slazengers Ltd., Challenge House, Mitcham Road, Croydon, Surrey, CR9 3AU.

If there's a good chance of getting the game established at school, consider these tips to avoid an over-high annual renewal cost of specialist padder bases and nets:

(1) Permanent metal playground sockets, with lids.
(2) Fitted metal posts, cut to 36 in. lengths, with one end plugged to take a 2 in. peg or spike for the net.
(3) Coloured nylon cord or string to replace the padder net to reduce cost and simply to provide a centre-court objective at correct height to hit over.
(4) Permanently painted playground court markings (Education Authorities have local firms on contract for this work).

This is an ideal game to start building-up in the Primary and Junior schools, where the basic skills and rules should be taught (but not over-done). In this way, an excellent foundation would be laid for the further development of first-class tennis with boys and girls over 12 years of age.

Padder-tennis gives pleasure at either singles or doubles and is probably one of the least understood, most neglected bat and ball games in schools, clubs and sports centres. It is much cheaper to set-up than regular tennis: the bats for a start are less than

Selected Tennis Activities

one-third the price of an ordinary tennis racket, and the balls do not have to be of such high quality, the padder bats being of laminated wood throughout. Perhaps it is the very nature of the equipment, being seemingly inferior to lawn tennis, that causes people to view the game in a disparaging sort of way, if they know of it at all, which is doubtful. Yet once a person has been introduced to padder-tennis and got stuck into the game, he is invariably hooked because its appeal is so strong.

It has all the interest, excitement and exercise value of ordinary tennis, yet is much, much easier to learn and play. This is because the wooden bat is so much easier to handle and control and the court is smaller. Yet all the strokes are there to be enjoyed: forehand-backhand, volleys, smash, half-volleys (if you are prepared to go down that low with this short-handled bat and you have to), chop, chip and slice... the only stroke that isn't on is the conventional overhead serve as in tennis. With padder the serve is made by either first dropping the ball in front of your front foot, or serving direct from the free hand below waist height into the diagonally opposite service court.

The bat, being short-handled (a mere $5\frac{1}{2}$ in. shank, with a $7\frac{1}{2}$ in. x 10 in. blade), offers no difficulty in handling and control to any age group, however young. It's particularly kind to weak muscles. Therefore, the newcomer to the game quickly gains great confidence in playing it.

Even so, this isn't to say that instruction and coaching is not needed, it most certainly is. I have witnessed many times, padder-tennis emerging at two entirely different levels: one as a kind of no-account play-about activity, that no one took seriously, because its organisers treated it as if it didn't need any serious consideration, just using it as a convenience activity to baby-mind awkward pupils.

Then again I've seen it given the full professional teaching treatment (not very common) and as a result, it has emerged as very popular, vigorously competitive and immensely worth-while as a serious bat and ball game in its own right. When you witness this latter, then you know a proper teaching job has been done. The happy, vigorous kids playing games and sets are proof.

It's a real treat to see the regular, recognised strokes being used as they were meant – with skilful, serious intent and very

Tennis for Schools

obvious enjoyment. I personally feel very pleased to be responsible for introducing this experience to many hundreds of London's East Enders, when they were at school and making the most of their all too short weekly games ration.

Summary on Padder-tennis

* The nearest, realistic game to lawn tennis, but played on hard courts, or in sports halls or gyms, not grass.

* All its strokes (except service) are the same as tennis, and should be given that treatment, never just glossed over as if they didn't count. They do.

* The serve is either direct from the free hand from below the waist; or by first dropping the ball to bounce in front of the leading foot.

* The rules are the same as tennis (or the edited version that is used). To be realistic, there's no need to pedantically insist on sticking to every tennis rule you can find. You don't want to slow the game down.

* Line and net judging and scoring does require discipline and and firm adherence to the rules. Treat it like tennis.

* *Grips and bat handling:* give this every bit the same respect and serious consideration that you would tennis. Never give in to a momentary laziness and drop the head of the bat to scope up low balls instead of bending the knees and getting down to them properly. Keep that bat head wrist high.

* Think of padder as being an excellent substitute for tennis for younger children, principally because the bat is so much easier to control, especially as it has such a short handle

* On this basis, seize every opportunity to get padder-tennis started with the Primary and Junior classes.

* But, never imagine that older folk won't take to the game. They will and do, with real enthusiasm. Here again, no doubt it's mainly because they can turn that smaller bat into a natural extension of their striking arm and make it perform exactly as they wish.

Selected Tennis Activities

* The equipment may be difficult to locate and purchase, according to what part of the country you operate from. This is why I named the manufacturers of the posts, nets and bats. There are other suppliers, but not many. Here are three more, in case you get stuck:

Posts and bases: Lillywhite Frowd Ltd.,   and at:
Sports Goods Manufacturers,   18 Mora Street,
P.O. Box No. 1,   London E.C1.
Medway Wharf Road,
Tonbridge, TN9 1QJ.

Peter Pan Manufacturing
Company,
Sun Street,
Brierley Hill,
Staffordshire.

Nets: Bridport Gundry,
Bridport,
Dorset.

Galvanised posts: Singer & James Ltd.,
Roebuck Road,
Hainault,
Ilford,
Essex.

Write and ask them for a catalogue. There'll be lots of other items of interest.

* Sorry if you think I have short-changed you a bit on actual information on rules and method of play. In fact, published data of this sort on padder-tennis is practically non-existent. But that shouldn't worry you, the game is *played and scored like tennis*.

24

Fitness
The right game can make you fit, but you also need to be fit for the game

Cynics of the fitness game

This is a fact of life we can't ignore, or want to. It's just that many (most?) people find the acquiring of it too much trouble to make the effort. Except when you're in the business of inspiring and educating others towards healthier living, or at least improved performance in sport, fitness can't be overlooked.

The whole point is, finding some enjoyable, motivation that will stimulate us into *wanting to make the effort* to get fit. And this is the crux of it: *fit for what?*

Fit for what?

In our case there's no doubt. It's going to be fit for tennis. Fit for playing it and teaching it, with the extra incentive of wanting to give our pupils the benefit of our experience and feeling fulfilment when they catch-on and start developing strong, quick, attractive bodies. Athletes of the tennis court are wonderfully graceful persons that make it seem all meaningful and worthwhile.

But you can't expect to get and enjoy that fine edge of fitness just by playing tennis alone. For a start, it's a one-sided sport. Who wants one side of their body larger and stronger than the other? Then there's the inner, unseen fitness factor to develop – *cardiovascular fitness,* probably the most important fitness factor of all.

In these days of increasingly mechanised, sedentary living the heart and circulation are the most grossly neglected part of the human body. (The belly and bowels the most over-worked!)

Tennis could take care of all that for us – as long as we pay heed to that one-sided aspect, overcome it and get fit all over.

'TV Bottom, Loafer's Heart' and school P.E.

Nowadays, physically, there seems to be more and more inclination to relax, recline and take it easy; which is unarguably contrary to good muscle-tone, stress-free posture and a healthy, fit circulo-respiratory system.

As a direct result of this easy-way-living attitude, fitness tests for Army, Navy, Air Force and police recruits and cadets, have revealed lack of development and strength in the upper-body and abdominal muscles.

Weakness was particularly noticeable in the arm and shoulder-girdle musculature, together with a deficiency in general muscular and physiological endurance. This was revealed in their failure to lift or push their body-weight off the ground (rope climbs and push-ups); and failed running tests for cardiovascular fitness.

This bodily failing in modern, machine-age man makes the schools' physical education programme all the more vital as means of showing the way and creating a desire for improved physical fitness and well-being.

One thing is certain: schools' physical education can no longer be lightly treated as merely a semi-serious subject of 'fun and games'. It most certainly must concern itself with the vitally-urgent problem of physical survival in a chaotic environment of plastics, chemicals, machines, robots, computers, automation and over-population.

The P.E. teacher from the 1970s must be equipped mentally, physically and professionally to grasp hold of and deal decisively with this increasing problem of unfitness, to tackle it through the impressionable minds and malleable bodies of his or her young pupils.

Physical inactivity is becoming our modern malady. The only antidote is regular daily exercise of a sufficiently massive nature to stimulate heart, circulation, lungs, glandular, digestive and excretory systems, and to maintain firm muscle-tone and joint flexibility.

Tennis for Schools

Fitness and survival through physical education must be universally accepted as the common denominator of the majority, not merely the privilege of the athletic few. This is why tennis can be so valuable in schools, because of its joint fun appeal and exercise potential, provided it is supplemented with other forms of training to balance out its one-sided shortcomings.

What is fitness?

It is a fluctuating, dynamic process of health and functional efficiency, maintained at optimum levels by *regular daily use,* but degenerates rapidly by neglect of this day-to-day application.

It is an organic-structural, biochemical condition that cannot be stored up like food, money or knowledge in a kind of fitness bank. Nothing is lost so quickly as fitness if it is not used regularly and maintained constantly. A truism not likely to appeal to an anti-physical man. But the inescapable fact remains; fitness is here, but not to stay, unless we choose.

Fitness requires effort, if it is to exist at all. This we have to know, believe and accept unquestionably as essential to the human condition as eating and sleeping. It really is no good kidding ourselves that there is any other way. I'm not even willing to concede that it can come under the category of 'options' in a P.E. programme. In fact, I'm sure it can't.

So now, to be truly fit, a person should strive to maintain an alert, enquiring mind, emotional stability, and combine outstanding mental qualities with bodily development, strength, agility, endurance and the aesthetic appeal of physical beauty. And if someone wants to criticise this as being an impossible and unobtainable ideal, let him stand naked in front of a full-length mirror and be honestly satisfied and proud of what he sees!

Measurable factors

Now to get down to business. Leaving out all the generalisations on fitness, in our context of tennis, we've got to relate fitness as a condition that is practical, functional, workable, enjoyable and inseparable from playing skilful, competitive, worthwhile games. So we can recognise and assess its effects by these 'fitness factors' in the following terms:

Strength: the capacity to exert muscular force against a resistance (measured in the gym or fitness lab by dynamometers). The ability to push or pull heavy loads and lift heavy weight.

Muscular Endurance: the ability of isolated muscle-groups to resist fatigue and keep working under the pressure of continuous localised use, such as 'chinning' a bar, push-ups, 'dipping' between parallel bars-; or practical work such as using a foot pump on tyres, sandpapering paint-work, sawing logs.

Cardiovascular-respiratory Endurance: this involves the whole body through the heart, blood-vessels and lungs. It is a measure of their ability to function continuously under a heavy workload in activity involving *total body movement* of a *massive* nature, such as soccer, rugby, swimming, distance running, hard tennis sets, basketball, hill-climbing, etc. It is assessed by medical scientists and professional coaches to be the most important of all the fitness factors.

Power: the capacity to develop an *explosive* rate of work. When measured in foot pounds per second, it reveals the product of *force* plus *velocity*. It shows a person's ability to propel his own body or some other object rapidly through space, e.g. high and long jumping, throwing the discus, shot or javelin, sprinting (particularly the start), pole-vaulting, bowling a ball, jumping high to head a soccer ball, serving an 'ace' in tennis and delivering powerful ground strokes!

Development and Posture: the muscle structure in relationship to fat, bone formation and height, and its co-ordinated carriage and poise. This comparison emphasises physical beauty, balance, harmony and eye-appeal. We recognise these qualities in animals, birds and fishes instantly, although we seem to have differing standards about humans!

Flexibility and Agility: here you have fitness exemplified by the top world soccer, rugby, hockey and skating stars in action and the greats of ballet and free-expressionist dance form, the top gymnasts and acrobats, divers, top basketball and tennis players. Or simply moving with grace and sensitivity about the normal acts of living (This is where the art of biodynamics comes in).

So these six fitness factors ought to be recognised as an irrefutable part of our living pattern, or life style. They certainly influence tennis enormously. If we are going to play it we need them.

Conversely: mechanised, sedentary, car-and-office-bound living drastically reduces flexibility, restricts joints, weakens, destroys and distorts muscle, and creates stiffness, twinges and premature old age. But once again, here's where tennis comes in: if we get a desire to play it, we shall most probably want to get our bodies fitter than they might normally be. In which case, we can have these fitness factors in our minds for utilisation. Tennis becomes the motivation.

Fitness in this context is concerned chiefly as it relates to actual physical training, conditioning, 'work-outs', or whatever description is popular.

With the concept of total or balanced fitness in mind, training activities can be designed to affect these major fitness factors and ensure overall balanced physical and physiological development *and* functional ability. We can become the real tigers of the tennis courts.

Applying fitness to tennis training

If a teacher or coach is convinced that a pupil's tennis performance is influenced and greatly improved by supplementing the basic skills and practices with fitness training, three factors need attention:

1. *Overcoming mental inertia* – the hardest part of many a training session at any age-level.
2. *Regularity to develop the habit for training* – but never allowing training to become just a habit! Each session should be a fresh and stimulating experience, never a boring routine. Each session for pupils should be an opportunity for intimate, possibly exciting body-awareness (Educational Gymnastics and Movement and Dance are our allies here).
3. *Relating fitness training to functional tennis*
   (a) Working-out exercises and activities to suit and influence specific tennis performance.
   (b) Pupils' awareness of the *reason why* they are performing certain exercises. Sharing the understanding with the teacher.

So when it comes to preparing training sessions, apart from figuring-out how to teach particular skills, techniques and tactics, we have to write into our programmes the specific fitness exercises that we believe will directly affect those skills and practices. We bear in mind something like this:

(c) Relate the particular tennis skill with anatomical physiological requirement and write the specific fitness training into the lesson.
(d) Study the Fitness Factors to see precisely which factor relates to the particular tennis skill: e.g. *serving* requires *flexibility* and *power*.
(e) *Muscular* and *cardiovascular endurance* are basic to general tennis performance, so write-in the appropriate fitness exercises to *each* leasson.

Skills and fitness guide
Tennis skill – fitness factors – sample exercise

GRIP

Flexibility: flexion-extension of fingers and wrist, rotation of wrists. (Stretching-mobilising).

Strength: rope-climb, parallel bars, weight-training, medicine-ball throwing, pull-ups, squeezing a ball.

GROUNDSTROKES, VOLLEYS, LOBS

Strength: as for grip, plus push-ups, handstands, hand-walking, 'wheelbarrows', front-support wrestling, amateur wrestling.

SERVICE AND SMASH

Strength: as for grip and groundstrokes, plus additional exercises that prove suitable.

Flexibility: as for grip, plus free-arm circling, shoulder rotation, conscious relaxation and release of tension in the shoulder joint (stretching-mobilising).

Tennis for Schools

Power: throwing a ball for distance and at targets; throwing shot, discus, javelin; maintain full flexion-extension of the elbow; good muscle-tone essential.

SCRAMBLING/FITNESS TO SUSTAIN ENDURANCE

Agility: skipping, hopping, squats, fast, half-squats from the 'spring-kneed' readiness position, crow-hops, 'carpet-jogging', Squash. (Stretching-mobilising-strengthening.)

Power: related to agility with similar exercise requirements, plus sprint-starts, sprinting, high-jumping, pole-vaulting.

Cardio-vascular-endurance running training (particularly middle and long-distance), 'carpet-jogging', jogging, swimming, soccer, rugby, hockey and similar total-body ball games to maintain condition of heart, circulation and lungs out of the tennis season. Progressively repeated sets of our familiar fast half-squats act as a muscular pump for venus return, so make sure to fit them into daily training.

SPECIAL NOTE: all supplementary exercise should be conducted on a total-body, two-sided basis, to balance out the onesided effect of continued use of the racket in tennis (or indeed squash and badminton).

There is no suggestion that these examples are complete, or even adequate: but simply to stimulate throught along these lines as a basis for possible training programmes specifically related to tennis.

Summary

* Tennis can be used, not just as an end in itself, but as a means for encouraging children to take an active interest in their own physical prowess and fitness.

* It is a fact that after their initial introduction of the warm-up, fitness-training and skills approach to a tennis session, boys have begun to understand why skills and fitness-training have to be an essential part of the lesson – or why it has to be a lesson at all and not merely a recreational period.

* It has been known for such boys to actually protest to the teacher at losing their preliminary training session, when he has suggested that 'Today we'll just go out and play tennis...' Obviously they had begun to appreciate what it is all about. Which is precisely our aim.

* The big difficulty with non-P.E. teachers taking games training sessions, is getting them convinced that *training* is the operative word, with fitness and skill-training, predominant. Presumably, it can be all too easy to take pupils out for an 'uncomplicated' recreational period (I won't call it a lesson). Teachers who do this with swimming periods are little more than 'pool-side squatters'!). Does this suggest we could be saddled with 'tennis-court minders'?

Reviewing some facts

* Physical activity is a growth stimulus.
* Physical fitness is a condition of totality, involving the internal factors of mental physical and emotional; influenced by the external factors of environmental and social.
* This concept of total fitness is achieved through: planned, balanced activity, regularity of exercise; sleep, rest and relaxation; disciplined, intelligent, selective eating of natural foods; recreation and play; emotional stability; simple, basic pleasure and enjoyment from exercise and play-activity.
* Fitness cannot be stored up like food or money, but must be continually renewed by using it.
* Children need approximately four hours of massive, big-muscle activity daily for healthy development.
* Fortunately, young children have as natural a compulsive urge for massive bodily movement as for food and sleep. It is our responsibility (teachers' and parents') to provide the

encouragement and the means to satisfy this basic childhood urge.

* Unfortunately, in modern towns and cities, children do not get the opportunity for as much big muscle activity as they need.

Tennis once more comes to the rescue. Tennis plus supplementary fitness training would appear to be just the acceptable activity our young folk can welcome to improve their physical condition while enjoying the incentive of fun and games.

Supplementary home-fitness training

A. Teacher gives pupils weekly exercise assignment and they keep their own record in a personal fitness book – periodically checked.

B. *Basic body training session:*

* 'Carpet jogging' (minimum 300 reps.).
* Jogging mileage daily (minimum 2 miles).
* Push-ups (minimum 12).
* Pull-up (minimum 12). Modified for girls.
* Jack-knife leg lifts (minimum 12).
* Torso-twists (minimum 12).

NOTE: this is the barest minimum work-out for keen, athletic types; but also shouldn't discourage the more sluggish characters.

The '3 × 15' exercise theory

There is some promotion now among a few researchers and cardiac specialists, for a 'three times a week' exercise policy. Based upon their investigation of patients suffering from cardio-vascular malfunctioning, these specialists claim that a supplementary exercise programme of only 15 minutes, three times weekly, is sufficient to cause a noticeable improvement in the patients' heart condition. Conversely, such a programme would

Fitness

Daily Maintenance Work-out

Fig. 45. Personal fitness training for tennis

NOTE: this is a little daily, personal work-out that a boy or girl can do at home to improve over-all fitness for tennis. Included with it should be an exercise for cardiovascular fitness (heart, blood-vessels and lungs). 'Carpet jogging' for a planned number of reps. is ideal. (*Physical Fitness for Boys* by the author: Pelham Books, 1972.)

have a most beneficial *preventive* effect for anyone who may otherwise have had a predisposition towards heart failure.

This 'Three times fifteen' exercise policy, may seem ludicrously inadequate to people who believe in training vigorously every day to maintain a high level of fitness. And of course it is, to competitive athletes, professional sportsmen and sportswomen and the like. But let us not confuse the physical requirements of these athletes with the soft physical condition of unexercised, sedentary people.

The anti-physical persons, who may overeat and also suffer stress, are the kind most likely to be predisposed towards deterioration and failure of their cardio-respiratory systems. These are the very ones who can most benefit by this 3 x 15 exercise proposal.

Schoolboys and girls however, and athletically-inclined persons in particular, need greater exercise stimulation of their circulo-respiratory and muscular systems for a noticeable improvement in their fitness for competitive sport. In their case, a daily maintenance work-out, or alternatively, a three times weekly, total body training session based upon the main fitness factors is appropriate. And this could not be effectively achieved in fifteen minutes!

On the other hand, using this 3 x 15 scheme as a supplementary training programme to their regular school physical education, could be a most practical, attractive and acceptable policy. It's an idea.

Further reading and study (*particularly for exercisse and activities*)

Aids to Tennis Teaching by W. G. Moss, national coach for lawn tennis in Scotland (A. Learmonth & Sons, 9 Kings Street, Stirling, Scotland). Available from: Secretary, Scottish Lawn Tennis Association, 1 Royal Terrace, Edinburgh, EH7 5AD. Price 20p (including postage).

Lawn Tennis Group Coaching, compiled by The Girls' Schools' Lawn Tennis Association (approved by the L.T.A.). Obtainable from: Miss M. E. Parker, 'Cobbler's, East Shalford Lane, Shalford, Guildford, Surrey. Price 15p post paid.

Tennis Practices and Exercises, and *A Tennis Professional's Note-*

book, both by Dudley Georgeson, L.T.A. Registered Coach. Obtainable from: 54 Lyndhurst Gardens, Finchley, London, N3. Price 20p post paid.

(for fitness)

Physical Fitness For Schools, 1971. £2 *Physical Fitness For Boys*, 1972 £1.90. By Harcourt Roy (Pelham Books, London).
Live with Harcourt Roy (Thorsons Publishers, Denington Estate London Road, Wellingborough, Northants NN8 2RQ. 1969) £1.05.
Be Fit! Or Be Damned! by Percy Cerutty (Pelham Books, London. 1967).
The New Aerobics by Kenneth H. Cooper, M.D., author of Aerobics. (M. Evans and Company, Inc., New York. 1970) $5.95.
Improvements in Cardiovascular Condition of Humans Associated with Physical Training, Persistently Performed Sports and Exercises by Thomas K. Cureton (Physical Fitness Institute, University of Illinois, 141 Armory Building, Champaign, Illinois, 61820, U.S.A.).

Part Four
Helpful Comment and Information

Progress from the P.E. class to the school's tennis club and then the team. But after-school and weekend play is essential for real improvement, as a member of the local club, or on the public courts with a better player. Then lose no time in entering for tournaments around the district. This is how to improve, to be noticed, to attract professional coaching – and to feel that it is all worth while!

Problems with School Tennis

The Common Headache: Balls

(1) *Lost balls:* schools that make pupils pay for the balls they lose end up with fewer losses – but plenty of pupils afraid to play tennis! They will stand around, or pat the ball to each other cautiously or timidly, instead of developing vigorous, attacking tennis.

(2) *Balls on roofs:* in girls' schools at least, that's where the balls have to stay. The girls are not allowed to climb up to retrieve them, for fear of accident and injury (rightly so). No doubt the same ruling applies to boys as well; but teachers generally look the other way when there are so many willing 'drainpipe athletes' ready at the blink of an eye to do what boys have always done – climb up on to the roof. Back to the girls: if the schoolkeeper has a weak heart, or the weather is especially bad, he's not too keen on retrieving rooftop balls either. Can you blame him?

(3) *Marking balls:* this ought to be done without fail. But is it? Are there schoolkeepers with the will to do it, or staff members with time?

(4) *Expensive balls:* some P.E. departments complain that they can't get enough balls to last the year because of the expense. 'When these few dozen are used up or lost, that's our lot – and that's the end of tennis 'till next year!'

(5) *Cheaper balls:* firms do supply cheap tennis balls for school and club practice. It pays to locate this source of supply and start ordering by the several gross to see your classes through a year of regular instruction and practice. But beware some cheap makes: they either lose their nap within the week, or else the 'fur' becomes tatty and stringy and generally unpleasant. Apply your selectivity; but a regular supply of several gross you must have, to cover the hours of mass instruction and practice the pupils need.

(6) *Ball hazards:* these are the badly-planned courts, like the ones surrounded by trees, shrubs or flowerbeds; or located too

Tennis for Schools

close to school buildings or roadways – all obviously hazardous to wildly-hit balls – and you're going to be plagued with a neverending swarm of these. Although competent pre-competition skill-training under vigilant supervision will reduce this wild hitting.

(7) *Long-life balls:* these are the sort used on courts surrounded by space. Not that you have much say in the initial siting of the school's tennis courts; but plenty of surrounding space is preferable – for the balls' sake. At least, stray balls can then be more easily spotted and retrieved. This has actually been proved, in the field as it were.

Equal Status for Tennis

All too often, from the teacher-equipment-numbers-space point of view, tennis is classed as a minor sport in the overall P.E. programme. This is because its ratio of pupil numbers to available space is unbalanced and uneconomical. Teachers (or the Administration), may feel that the expensive court and equipment outlay required isn't justified by the limited number of children occupied (the same thing arises with school golf and archery).

This is where it becomes so important for P.E. departments to devise practical, mass instructional methods, making maximum use of sports hall and tennis court with the maximum number of pupils at one time. If 100 per cent of each school year can be adequately instructed and practised in the major team sports, without question, then tennis must be given equal status and included, as a regular, P.E. activity for every boy and girl.

Young Children and Tennis

(1) Tennis is not an easy game for young children to learn efficiently. The racket can be unwieldy and often is, until the under-developed muscles have become strong, trained and disciplined enough to dominate and dictate the stroke-play naturally. This is why padder-tennis is such a good lead-up game for small beginners with weaker arm muscles. The padder-bat is a more natural and easily managed extension of the child's arm, particularly with its short handle, but light, plywood head.

(2) Untutored children use their rackets like shovels, their most

common stroke being the underarm, upward shovelling action. Consequently, they spend unnecessary time collecting stray balls from the other side of the back fence.

'How long does it take to teach a youngster to keep the head of his racket up, rather than him dropping the racket head down and scooping the *ball* up? In fact, they've got to be taught to bend their knees and get down to the ball. Granted, the getting down takes effort.' These comments drop in my lap.

(3) This brings in the value of using a *low net* (like a padder net) at first. Try using a net below regulation height until stroke production is reasonably good. For example, don't wind the regulation net up tight, keep it slack at first to encourage beginners.

(4) Left to themselves, it is hard to believe they will naturally develop the standard strokes for skilled play. Nor are they likely to pay conscious heed to stance, foot placement and body positioning to achieve the most efficient action. That is, if they are left alone just for a bit of fun and amusement. On the other hand, by instinctive response, they may, by trial and error, develop a style of their own that makes use of a form of compensatory stroke-play, that may by chance resemble some of the standard strokes. Perhaps this is synonymous with the limited 'fun' noise of the pop group, compared with the skilled repertoire of the highly-trained, disciplined musician. Here we are up against the controversial issue of direct teaching versus self-discovery. A hot potato!

The Handicap of 'Options'

The free choice system of 'Options' given to older pupils from the fourth year upwards, and even third years in some schools, could encourage dabbling instead of learning and concentration. 'What would you like to do this term, boys?' Theoretically, it's a good progressive tactic; but it takes teachers with real merit and flair to see it through successfully. Teachers are still necessary.

In some schools, this can be a serious problem with many new and exciting sports being offered to younger and younger children (golf, archery, horse-riding, sailing, roller-skating), while actual standards of performance are dropping over the total number of participants. Fortunately, some pupils emerge willing to apply themselves and show a desire to improve their performance. These are the teachers' bonus!

But now that the policy of compulsion (and even direct teaching) has largely faded from contemporary P.E. fashion, some sports are suffering greatly diminished pupil support, while many newly introduced ones are being 'experienced'.

So what about tennis? We hope P.E. departments will be able to keep a careful eye on tennis in their yearly curriculum. Will there be sufficient time and equipment allocated to it as an *essential part* of the actual P.E. instruction programme? More to the point, will there be sufficient teachers willing and able to promote and instruct it, seriously? (Don't believe I think it shouldn't be fun!)

Motivating Pupils to Apply Themselves?

An old problem, for any subject. But with sport, the layman would say there shouldn't be any problem at all, because all kids love doing it. But we in the 'trade' are constantly at odds with both pupils and ourselves over this very problem of who wants to do what?

Throw them a ball and let them get on with it? Will this satisfy them for a whole period, keep them reasonably under control? Or, more in line with our professional consciences: should we push serious, planned, disciplined and progressive training, with maybe a game towards the end of the session, if they have earnt it? Or is this out-dated now?

The P.E. teacher might say: 'Where's the problem? If I'm going to include tennis in the curriculum, then they're going to learn it, properly. So what's your worry?'

Well, I go for that. They apply themselves and learn. But it's not as simple as that. Nowadays we are up against the self-discovery approach and teachers who still believe in and practise 'direct teaching' may be viewed askance by progressive colleagues. Yet, the old pendulum may swing back before we're through.

So it seems the problem is not what to teach, but how to offer it so that the pupils will accept it!

So we think hard: how to present tennis to pupils so they will 'take to it' eagerly and apply themselves seriously for improved performance? This is what we want them to do, improve their skills and ability? So back to the beginning. What is the motivation? Fun, of course.

But despite the current out-moded approach of direct teaching, please let there be direct and regular tennis instruction – for all. Even if it has to be compulsory! Unless, of course, the pupils aren't keen on it! Then what?

I should imagine this calls for as serious an examination and analysis of the teacher as much as anything. Delicate ground!

Rules of Lawn Tennis

(Approved by the International Lawn Tennis Federation 12th July 1972, when Rule 3 was amended.)

Reprinted here by kind permission of The Lawn Tennis Association, Barons Court, West Kensington, London, W14 9EG.

The singles game

1.—The Court shall be a rectangle, 78 ft. (23.77 m.) long and 27 ft. (8.23 m.) wide It shall be divided across the middle by a net, suspended from a cord or metal cable of a maximum diameter of third of an inch (.8 cm.), the ends of which shall be attached to, or pass over, the tops of two posts, 3 ft. 6 in. (1.07 m.) high, the centre of which shall be 3 ft. (0.91 m.) outside the Court on each side. The height of the net shall be 3 ft. (0.914 m.) at the centre, where it shall be held down taut by a strap not more than 2 in. (5 cm.) wide. There shall be a band covering the cord or metal cable and the top of the net for not less than 2 in. (5 cm.) nor more than $2\frac{1}{2}$ in. (6.3 cm.) in depth on each side. The lines bounding the ends and sides of the Court shall respectively be called the Base-lines and the Side-lines. On each side of the net, at a distance of 21 ft. (6.40 m.) from it and parallel with it, shall be drawn the Service-lines. The space on each side of the net between the service-line and the side-lines shall be divided into two equal parts called the service-courts by the centre service-line, which must be 2 in. (5 cm.) in width, drawn half-way between, and parallel with, the side-lines. Each base-line shall be bisected by an imaginary continuation of the centre service-line to a line 4 in. (10 cm.) in length and 2 in. (5 cm.) in width called the centre mark drawn inside the Court, at right angles to and in contact with such base-lines. All other lines shall be not less than 1 in. (2.5 cm.) nor more than 2 in. (5 cm.), in width, except the base-line, which may be 4 in. (10 cm.) in width, and all measurements shall be made to the outside of the lines.

Rules of Lawn Tennis

NOTE. – *In the case of the International Lawn Tennis Championship (Davis Cup) or other Official Championships of the International Federation, there shall be a space behind each baseline of not less than 21 ft. (6.4 m.), and at the sides of not less than 12 ft. (3.66 m.).*

2.—The permanent fixtures of the Court shall include not only the net, posts, cord or metal cable, strap and band, but also, where there are any such, the back and side stops, the stands, fixed or movable seats and chairs round the Court, and their occupants, all other fixtures around and above the Court, and the Umpire, Net-cord Judge, Foot-fault Judge, Linesmen and Ball Boys when in their respective places.

NOTE.—*For the purpose of this Rule, the word 'Umpire' comprehends the Umpire, the persons entitled to a seat on the Court, and all those persons designated to assist the Umpire in the conduct of a match.*

3.—The ball shall have a uniform outer surface and shall be white or yellow in colour. If there are any seams they shall be stitchless. The ball shall be more than two and a half inches (6.35 cm.) and less than two and five-eighths inches (6.67 cm.) in diameter, and more than two ounces (56.7 grams) and less than two and one-sixteenth ounces (58.5 grams) in weight. The ball shall have a bound of more than 53 in. (135 cm.) and less than 58 in. (147 cm.) when dropped 100 inches (254 cm.) upon a concrete base. The ball shall have a forward deformation of more than .220 of an inch (.56 cm.) and less than .290 of an inch (.74 cm.) and a return deformation of more than .350 of an inch (.89 cm.) and less than .425 of an inch (1.08 cm.) at 18 lb. (8.165 kg.) load. The two deformation figures shall be the averages of three individual readings along three axes of the ball and no two individual readings shall differ by more than .030 of an inch (.08 cm.) in each case. All tests for bound, size and deformation shall be made in accordance with the Regulations in the Appendix hereto.

4.—The players shall stand on opposite sides of the net; the player who first delivers the ball shall be called the Server, and the other the Receiver.

Tennis for Schools

5.—The choice of sides and the right to be Server or Receiver in the first game shall be decided by toss. The player winning the toss may choose or require his opponent to choose:
  (*a*) The right to be Server or Receiver, in which case the other player shall choose the side; or
  (*b*) The side, in which case the other player shall choose the right to be Server or Receiver.

6.—The service shall be delivered in the following manner. Immediately before commencing to serve, the Server shall stand with both feet at rest behind (i.e. further from the net than) the base-line, and within the imaginary continuations of the centre-mark and side-line. The Server shall then project the ball by hand into the air in any direction and before it hits the ground strike it with his racket, and the delivery shall be deemed to have been completed at the moment of the impact of the racket and the ball. A player with the use of only one arm may utilize his racket for the projection.

7.—The Server shall throughout the delivery of the service:
  (*a*) Not change his position by walking or running.
  (*b*) Not touch, with either foot, any area other than that behind the base-line within the imaginary extension of the centre mark and side-line.

NOTE.—*The following interpretation of Rule 7 was approved by the International Federation on 9th July, 1958:—*
  7.—(*a*) *The Server shall not, by slight movements of the feet which do not materially affect the location originally taken up by him, be deemed 'to change his position by walking or running'.*
  (*b*) *The word 'foot' means the extremity of the leg below the ankle.*

8.—(*a*) In delivering the service the Server shall stand alternately behind the right and left Courts beginning from the right in every game. If service from a wrong half of the Court occurs and is undetected, all play resulting from such wrong service or services shall stand, but the inaccuracy of station shall be corrected immediately it is discovered.
  (*b*) The ball served shall pass over the net and hit the ground within the Service Court which is diagonally opposite, or upon

Rules of Lawn Tennis

any line bounding such Court, before the Receiver returns it.

9.—The Service is a fault: (*a*) If the Server commit any breach of Rules 6, 7 or 8; (*b*) If he miss the ball in attempting to strike it; (*c*) If the ball served touch a permanent fixture (other than the net, strap or band) before it hits the ground.

10.—After a fault (if it be the first fault) the Server shall serve again from behind the same half of the Court from which he served that fault, unless the service was from the wrong half, when, in accordance with Rule 8, the Server shall be entitled to one service only from behind the other half. A fault may not be claimed after the next service has been delivered.

11.—The Server shall not serve until the Receiver is ready. If the latter attempt to return the service, he shall be deemed ready. If, however, the Receiver signify that he is not ready, he may not claim a fault because the ball does not hit the ground within the limits fixed for the service.

12.—In all cases where a let has to be called under the rules, or to provide for an interruption to play, it shall have the following interpretations:
 (*a*) When called solely in respect of a service that one service only shall be replayed.
 (*b*) When called under any other circumstance, the point shall be replayed.

13.—The service is a let:
(*a*) If the ball served touch the net, strap or band, and is otherwise good, or, after touching the net, strap or band, touch the Receiver or anything which he wears or carries before hitting the ground.
(*b*) If a service or a fault be delivered when the Receiver is not ready (see Rule 11).

In case of a let, that particular service shall not count, and the Server shall serve again, but a service let does not annul a previous fault.

14.—At the end of the first game the Receiver shall become Server, and the Server Receiver; and so on alternately in all the subsequent games of a match. If a player serve out of turn, the player who ought to have served shall serve as soon as the

Tennis for Schools

mistake is discovered, but all points scored before such discovery shall be reckoned. If a game shall have been completed before such discovery, the order of service remains as altered. A fault served before such discovery shall not be reckoned.

15.—A ball is in play from the moment at which it is delivered in service. Unless a fault or a let be called it remains in play until the point is decided.

16.—The Server wins the point:
 (a) If the ball served, not being a let under Rule 13, touch the Receiver or anything which he wears or carries, before it hits the ground;
 (b) If the Receiver otherwise loses the point as provided by Rule 18.

17.—The Receiver wins the point (a) If the Server serve two consecutive faults; (b) If the Server otherwise lose the point as provided by Rule 18.

18.—A player loses the point if:
 (a) He fail, before the ball in play has hit the ground twice consecutively, to return it directly over the net [except as provided in Rule 22 (a) or (c)]; or
 (b) He return the ball in play so that it hits the ground, a permanent fixture, or other object, outside any of the lines which bound his opponent's Court [except as provided in Rule 22 (a) and (c)]; or
 (c) He volley the ball and fail to make a good return even when standing outside the Court; or
 (d) He touch or strike the ball in play with his racket more than once in making a stroke; or
 (e) He or his racket (in his hand or otherwise) or anything which he wears or carries touch the net, posts, cord or metal cable, strap or band, or the ground within his opponent's Court at any time while the ball is in play; or
 (f) He volley the ball before it has passed the net; or
 (g) The ball in play touch him or anything that he wears or carries, except his racket in hand or hands; or
 (h) He throws his racket at and hits the ball.

19.—If a player commits any act either deliberate or involuntary which, in the opinion of the Umpire, hinders his opponent

Rules of Lawn Tennis

in making a stroke, the Umpire shall in the first case award the point to the opponent, and in the second case order the point to be replayed.

20.—A ball falling on a line is regarded as falling in the Court bounded by that line.

21.—If the ball in play touch a permanent fixture (other than the net, posts, cord or metal cable, strap or band) after it has hit the ground, the player who struck it wins the point; if before it hits the ground his opponent wins the point.

22.—It is a good return:
 (a) If the ball touch the net, posts, cord or metal cable, strap or band, provided that it passes over any of them and hits the ground within the Court; or
 (b) If the ball, served or returned, hit the ground within the proper Court and rebound or be blown back over the net, and the player whose turn it is to strike reach over the net and play the ball, provided that neither he nor any part of his clothes or racket touch the net, posts, cord or metal cable, strap or band or the ground within his opponent's Court, and that the stroke be otherwise good; or
 (c) If the ball be returned outside the post, either above or below the level of the top of the net, even though it touch the post, provided that it hits the ground within the proper Court; or
 (d) If a player's racket pass over the net after he has returned the ball, provided the ball pass the net before being played and be properly returned; or
 (e) If a player succeeds in returning the ball, served or in play, which strikes a ball lying in the Court.

NOTE TO RULE 22.—*In a singles match, if, for the sake of convenience, a doubles Court be equipped with singles posts for the purpose of a singles game, then the doubles posts and those portions of the net, cord or metal cable and band outside such singles posts shall at all times be permanent fixtures, and are not regarded as posts or parts of the net of a singles game.*

A return that passes under the net cord between the singles and adjacent doubles post without touching either net cord, net or doubles post and falls within the area of play, is a good return.

Tennis for Schools

23.—In case a player is hindered in making a stroke by anything not within his control, except a permanent fixture of the Court, or except as provided for in Rule 19, a let shall be called.

24.—If a player wins his first point, the score is called 15 for that player; on winning his second point, the score is called 30 for that player; on winning his third point, the score is called 40 for that player, and the fourth point won by a player is scored game for that player except as below:

If both players have won three points, the score is called deuce; and the next point won by a player is scored advantage for that player. If the same player win the next point, he wins the game; if the other player wins the next point the score is again called deuce; and so on, until a player wins the two points immediately following the score at deuce, when the game is scored for that player.

25.—A player (or players) who first wins six games wins a set; except that he must win by a margin of two games over his opponent and where necessary a set shall be extended until this margin be achieved.

26.—The players shall change sides at the end of the first, third and every subsequent alternate game of each set, and at the end of each set unless the total number of games in such set be even, in which case the change is not made until the end of the first game of the next set.

27.—The maximum number of sets in a match shall be 5, or, where women take part, 3.

28.—Except where otherwise stated, every reference in these Rules to the masculine includes the feminine gender.

29.—In matches where an Umpire is appointed, his decision shall be final; but where a Referee is appointed, an appeal shall lie to him from the decision of an Umpire on a question of law, and in all such cases the decision of the Referee shall be final.

In matches where assistants to the Umpire are appointed (linesmen, net cord judges, foot-fault judges) their decisions shall be final on questions of fact. When such an assistant is unable to give a decision he shall indicate this immediately to the Umpire who shall give a decision. When an Umpire is unable to give a decision on a question of fact he shall order the point to be replayed.

In Davis Cup matches only, the decision of an assistant to the Umpire, or of the Umpire if the assistant is unable to make a decision, can be changed by the Referee, who may also authorise the Umpire to change the decision of an assistant or order a point to be replayed.

The Referee, in his discretion, may at any time postpone a match on account of darkness or the condition of the ground or the weather. In any case of postponement the previous score and previous occupancy of Courts shall hold good, unless the Referee and the players unanimously agree otherwise.

30.—Play shall be continuous from the first service till the match be concluded; provided that after the third set, or when women take part, the second set, either player is entitled to a rest, which shall not exceed 10 minutes, or in countries situated between Latitude 15 degrees North and Latitude 15 degrees South, 45 minutes and provided further that when necessitated by circumstances not within the control of the players, the Umpire may suspend play for such a period as he may consider necessary. If play be suspended and be not resumed until a later day the rest may be taken only after the third set (or when women take part the second set) of play on such later day, completion of an unfinished set being counted as one set. These provisions shall be strictly construed, and play shall never be suspended, delayed or interfered with for the purpose of enabling a player to recover his strength or his wind, or to receive instruction or advice. The Umpire shall be the sole judge of such suspension, delay or interference, and after giving due warning he may disqualify the offender.

NOTES:

(a) *Any Nation is at liberty to modify the first provision in Rule 30 or omit it from its regulations governing tournaments matches or competitions held in its own country, other than the International Lawn Tennis Championships (Davis Cup and Federation Cup).*

(b) *When changing sides a maximum of one minute shall elapse from the cessation of the previous game to the time players are ready to begin the next game.*

The doubles game

31.—The above Rules shall apply to the Doubles Game except as below.

32.—For the Doubles Game, the Court shall be 36 ft. (10.97 m.) in width, i.e. 4½ ft. (1.37 m.) wider on each side than the Court for the Singles Game, and those portions of the singles side-lines which lie between the two service-lines shall be called the service-side-lines. In other respects, the Court shall be similar to that described in Rule, 1, but the portions of the singles side-lines between the base-line and service-line on each side of the net may be omitted if desired.

33.—The order of serving shall be decided at the beginning of each set as follows:

The pair who have to serve in the first game of each set shall decide which partner shall do so and the opposing pair shall decide similarly for the second game. The partner of the player who served in the first game shall serve in the third; the partner of the player who served in the second game shall serve in the fourth, and so on in the same order in all the subsequent games of a set.

34.—The order of receiving the service shall be decided at the beginning of each set as follows:

The pair who have to receive the service in the first game shall decide which partner shall receive the first service, and that partner shall continue to receive the first service in every odd game throughout that set. The opposing pair shall likewise decide which partner shall receive the first service in the second game and that partner shall continue to receive the first service in every even game throughout that set. Partners shall receive the service alternately throughout each game.

35.—If a partner serve out of his turn, the partner who ought to have served shall serve as soon as the mistake is discovered, but all points scored, and any faults served before such discovery, shall be reckoned. If a game shall have been completed before such discovery, the order of service remains as altered.

36.—If during a game the order of receiving the service is changed by the receivers it shall remain as altered until the end

Rules of Lawn Tennis

of the game in which the mistake is discovered, but the partners shall resume their original order of receiving in the next game of that set in which they are receivers of the service.

37.—The service is a fault as provided for by Rule 9, or if the ball touch the Server's partner or anything which he wears or carries; but if the ball served touch the partner of the Receiver, or anything which he wears or carries, not being a let under Rule 13 (a) before it hits the ground, the Server wins the point.

38.—The ball shall be struck alternately by one or other player of the opposing pairs, and if a player touches the ball in play with his racket in contravention of this Rule, his opponents win the point.

NOTE: these rules are from the regular L.T.A. booklet issue to give the basic, practical requirement for the working teacher, coach and pupil. They have lost nothing as rules in their reproduction; only the following items have been omitted from the booklet: 'How To Mark Out A Court', 'Plan Of Courts', and 'Cases and Decisions'. These are certainly recommended to strengthen a person's tennis education, and can be bought from the L.T.A. For 10p (ten pence) inclusive with the booklet.

Like the Law, rules are useful when they are needed.

Major Competitions

We are principally concerned here with competitions organised for school pupils in Great Britain. In this we are most fortunate to have had the work of research and editing done for us by Mr J. Gordon Rae, a Councillor and member of the L.T.A., who lives in Lancashire. The pamphlet *Lawn Tennis Competitions for Schools* at the price of 10p per copy (post paid), is the result of his dedication, with special rates for 4, 10, 20, 50 copies or more. Orders direct from:

> Mr J. Gordon Rae,
> 91 Buncer Lane,
> Blackburn,
> Lancashire, BB2 6SN.

The contents of the pamphlet are here reproduced as edited and compiled by Mr Rae, and by his kind permission.

Lawn tennis competitions for schools

THE LAWN TENNIS ASSOCIATION is the governing body of the game in Great Britain and is constituted of representatives from all the County Lawn Tennis Associations of England, the Scottish L.T.A., the Welsh L.T.A., the L.T.A. of the three Services, the Civil Service L.T.A., the Lawn Tennis Clubs of Oxford and Croquet Club, and the Schools' Associations. In addition to belonging to any of the three Schools' Associations, of which details follow later, schools may be linked to the L.T.A. in the same way as clubs by affiliating to their respective County Association.

The Lawn Tennis Association runs two Schools' Competitions:
The Aberdare Cup for girls' schools.
The Glanvill Cup for boys' schools.

Major Competitions

Any school may enter a team of three pairs for doubles. Entries must be sent to the Secretary, The Lawn Tennis Association, Barons Court, London, W14 9EG. early in December in the previous year. The fee is 60p per team, reduced to 40p if the school is a member of its respective Girls' or Boys' Schools Association. Entries are divided among four areas, North, South, East and West, and in each area the first round is drawn so that a group of three or four schools from roughly the same locality all play against each other, and that school winning the most matches progresses to the second round of the knock-out tournament. The winning team from each area goes forward to the semi-finals and final in July, usually played on the Friday following the Wimbledon Championships.

The Aberdare Cup finals are played at the All England L.T.C., Wimbledon, and the Glanvill Cup finals at the Queen's Club, West Kensington; all on hard courts.

The Captain's Cup, presented by W. J. Greener, is held annually by the captain of the winning team in the Aberdare Cup.

THE PUBLIC SCHOOLS' LAWN TENNIS ASSOCIATION

The Hon. Secretary is A. L. Thomas, 3 Dry Hill Park Crescent, Tonbridge, Kent. Membership is open to schools who are represented on the Headmasters' Conference, and the affiliation fee is 75p per annum. Schools must also affiliate direct to their respective County L.T.A.

A Tennis Coaching Course for Masters is run every other year at the Crystal Palace National Recreation Centre, in conjunction with the Incorporated Association of Preparatory Schools.

The Public Schools' L.T.A. runs two schools' tournaments, with two plate competitions; entries close about the third week in May.

The Youll Cup is a knock-out tournament for teams of two pairs playing a 3-set doubles match against corresponding pairs. If the two matches are shared a deciding singles is played between nominated players from each team. In the later rounds both pairs play each other to produce a match of four rubbers, with the deciding singles if necessary. There are no preliminary competi-

Tennis for Schools

tions in localities, all matches being contested on the hard courts at the All England L.T.C., Wimbledon, during the third or fourth week of July. The entry fee is £4 per school

The Thomas Bowl is a knock-out junior tournament for school pairs under $15\frac{1}{2}$ years of age on the previous 31st of December. A school may enter a second pair as additional competitors if it so wishes, and the entry fee is 50p per pair. The matches are played concurrently with the Youll Cup, but at Aorangi Park the New Zealand Sports Club adjacent to the All England L.T.C.

The Clark Trophy is the plate competition for school pairs knocked out in the first round of the Youll Cup.

There is also a plate competition for pairs knocked out in the first round of the Thomas Bowl.

At the conclusion of Public Schools' week a team is selected to represent the Public Schools' L.T.A. against the All England L.T.C. This match is the only schools' event played on the grass courts at Wimbledon.

The Incorporated Association of Preparatory Schools is affiliated to the Public Schools' L.T.A. and runs what is commonly called—

'The Prep. Schools' Tournament', for which entries can only be made through the Headmaster of a preparatory school member of I.A.P.S. Entries are limited to four boys from schools of up to 150 boys and six from schools of over 150, and should be forwarded to the Hon. Secretary of the I.A.P.S. Tennis Committee, J. E. Vidal, The Old Ride, Bradford-on-Avon, Wiltshire, by mid-July. The entry fee is £1.50 per boy who is expected to play in both singles and doubles.

The tournament takes place during the last three days in the week of the Youll Cup, initially at three centres (Hurlingham Club, Roehampton Club, and Harrodian Club or nearby St Paul's School) each with a limit of 30 pairs.

On the Thursday at each centre six groups of five doubles pairs play an American tournament, and the winners and runners-up go into a knock-out competition reducing to two pairs.

On the Friday at each centre fifteen groups of four singles play off similarly reducing to four players. At this stage each match consists of one 'short set', each game being restricted to 3 deuce calls, the next point being called 'game', except at 5-all when a full advantage game is played.

Major Competitions

On the Saturday the 2 doubles pairs and 4 singles players remaining from each centre play an orthodox knock-out tournament on hard courts at the All England L.T.C. Wimbledon.

THE BOYS' SCHOOLS LAWN TENNIS ASSOCIATION

The Hon. Secretary is W. E. Curtis, Royal Hospital School, Ipswich, Suffolk. The affiliation fee is 50p per annum and schools must also affiliate to their respective County L.T.A. The Boys' Schools L.T.A. organises both regional and national coaching courses for boys, and coaching training courses for schoolmasters.

It runs the following championships open to all affiliated schools, filling a 5-day programme, and in every case the competition takes the same form. Teams consist of two boys who play two singles, and if the match then stands at 1-all a deciding doubles is played.

The Clark Cup is the senior competition for teams under the age of 19 years 4 months on the previous 31st of December, and is played on a knock-out basis on hard courts at the All England L.T.C., Wimbledon, in the second or third week of July.

The Milbourn Cup is the junior competition for teams under the age of 15 years 4 months on the previous 31st of December, and is played similarly and concurrently with the Clark Cup, the early rounds taking place on the public courts at Wimbledon Park.

The Ramsden Cup is a plate competition for teams knocked out in the first round of the Clark Cup.

The Cheetham Cup is a plate competition for teams knocked out in the first round of the Milbourn Cup.

Teams can be accommodated during these events at Southlands College, Wimbledon.

Entry forms are sent out to more than 400 affiliated schools with the January Bulletin, and the entry fees are £2.25 for one event or £3.50 for both events.

The Norris Haugh Special Trophy is awarded annually by the Hon. Referee to the school team who by their conduct and co-operation contribute most to the success of the tournament. It is a book, secure in a burnished gilding-metal container, in which the donor, who was Referee for many years, wrote the story how the trophy came into being; and each year his successor adds a citation in support of his award.

Five Regional Tournaments are also played on similar lines at various centres within the regions during the Summer Term, each in three groups—Under-20 years, Under-16 years, and Under-14 years on the 1st of September in that year. Entires must be sent to the Regional Hon. Secretaries:

North:	J. Coates, Hymers College, Hull, East Yorkshire.
East:	W. E. Curtis, Royal Hospital School, Ipswich, Suffolk.
South-West:	C. Paull, King Edward VI School, Totnes, Devon.
Midland:	B.Tomlinson, King Edwards School, Birmingham 15.
South:	D. Russell, Chichester High School, Chichester, Sussex.

Regional plate competitions are also run for teams knocked out in the first rounds.

Winning teams from each of the five regional tournaments play off against the other winning teams in their age group, to decide the overall winning School from all the regions. These inter-regional finals are played on hard courts at Wimbledon during the B.S.L.T.A. Wimbledon Week.

The Association helps with the fares and pays for the accommodation at Southlands College of all teams playing in the inter-regional finals.

THE GIRLS' SCHOOLS LAWN TENNIS ASSOCIATION

The Hon. Secretary is Miss M. E. Parker, Cobblers, East Shalford Lane, Guildford, Surrey. Membership is open to all secondary, comprehensive and grammar schools, who must also affiliate to their respective County L.T.A. The affiliation fee is 50p per annum, with an entry fee of 13p.

The main work of the Girls' Schools L.T.A. lies in organising some forty coaching courses at centres during the Easter holidays. It has published the 'Group Coaching Pamphlet', over 4,000 copies having been sold at 15p, and each term circulates a

Major Competitions

bulletin on all tennis matters to all 800 member schools. The G.S.L.T.A. enjoys a generous allocation of Wimbledon tickets.

No school tournaments are run but the Association supports the L.T.A. in the Aberdare Cup, the L.T.F. in the Nestlé Schools' Tournament, and the Queen's Club in the Schoolgirls' Tournament.

The Queen's Club Schoolgirls' Tournament is open to any schoolgirl who must not have left school before the Summer term. Entries must be sent to the Secretary, The Queen's Club, West Kensington, W.14, by the first week of July, and the tournament, which consists of both singles and doubles in two age groups, is played wholly at the Queen's Club on hard courts during the last week of July. Partners in doubles need not belong to the same school. The entry fee is 60p for singles and 40p for each player in doubles.

The Yatman Cup is the senior singles event, limited to 128 players.

The Watt Bowl is a singles event for girls under 16 years on the previous 1st of January, and is limited to 64 players.

The Courtauld Cup is the senior doubles event, limited to 64 pairs.

There is also a doubles under 16 event limited to 32 pairs.

Competitors may not compete in both singles or both doubles.

THE LAWN TENNIS FOUNDATION is a non-profit making organisation supported by a number of firms commercially interested in promoting the playing of the game particularly among young people. In addition to supplying information on how, when and where to play, setting up coaching centres and demonstrations, and advising the great National Youth Organisations in tennis matters, the L.T.F. administers the largest schools' tournament in the world:

The Nestlé Schools Ladder Tournament, sponsored by The Nestlé Company, involves well over 32,000 boys and girls in schools in the four countries England, Ireland, Scotland and Wales. Each country runs its own boys' and girls' tournaments, on similar lines, and stages its own National Finals. The eight winners progress to the International Finals, immediately following the English National Finals, at the Queen's Club, West Kensington.

Tennis for Schools

Schools must obtain entry forms by early May from their national organiser.

England and Wales: Jack Moore, Manager, The Lawn Tennis Foundation, The Queen's Club, West Kensington, W.14.

Scotland: J. Blain, 91 Munro Road, Jordanhill, Glasgow, W.3.

Ireland: C. J. Brennan, Villa Maria, 15 Cill Eanna, Rahney, Dublin 5.

The tournament is played in two parts, and is open to any schoolboy or schoolgirl who, at the date of entry, has NOT played in the singles event of the Junior Championships of Great Britain. There is no age grouping, and singles only are played.

I. The Schools' Ladder Tournament, is generated by ladder boards, each accommodating from 8 to 24 players, being issued to schools who enter the tournament at an entry fee of 50p per ladder. There is no limit to the number of ladders a school may take. The board is 'played' according to the rules over a six weeks period between the date of entry and the end of June. Matches in this tournament consist of one 'short set', and are played at the school or in local parks and clubs. A player may challenge, within a time limit of 3 days, either of the two players immediately above him on the ladder, and if he wins he exchanges positions with the loser. The winner of the ladder, or the next nearest the top should the winner not be available, is invited to represent his or her school in the second part of the tournament.

II. The Schools' Knock-out Tournament, which has in the meantime been set up by putting into a draw every ladder which has been issued to schools, now takes finite form when all the schools are invited to nominate (with home address and telephone number) the winner of each ladder, the player so named going into the orthodox regional knock-out tournament. In pursuit of economy the country is divided into five areas, North, South, East, West and Midlands, and each such area into four regions. The original draw has been made, by ladders, for each of the twenty regions so formed. Each match is the best of three advantage sets and is played by mutual arrangement after opponents have been notified. Players report the result to the L.T.F., or national organiser, an dthe winner is then told who is his next opponent and by when the round must be played. Any excess over 50p incurred in second class rail fares may be claimed from the L.T.F. The twenty players who emerge as winners in

Major Competitions

each region are put in the draw for the National Finals, which (in the English event) are played on hard courts at the Queen's Club, West Kensington, in mid-September.

Prizes. All players who are at the top of a ladder at the end of the ladder-playing period receive a prize; and money grants are made to the schools playing the most ladder matches, and to the school taking the grestest number of ladders.

The Nestlé Trophy is awarded for one year to the winners of the National tournament, together with a Plaque, a prize voucher, and inclusion in the international event.

The Nestlé Schools Shield is awarded for one year to the schools he and she represent.

There are proportionate second, third, fourth and fifth prizes for players and their schools.

The Nestlé International Tournament consists of semi-finals and final for the four boy winners and the four girl winners of the National tournaments. Each year the title carries awards and privileges befitting the boy and girl who have first topped a school ladder and then had to win a possible maximum of 13 consecutive matches.

Major British and International Championships

It is logical to include this list for general (or specific) information, but also because our pupils need additional encouragement and motivation. Knowledge of national tournaments can help bring them more fully into the tennis theme.

The International Lawn Tennis Championship (*Davis Cup*)
Ladies International Team Championship (*Federation Cup*)
H.M. King Gustaf V of Sweden Cup (*King's Cup*)
Great Britain v. United States of America (*Wightman Cup*)
The Hard Court Championships of Great Britain
The Covered Court Championships of Great Britain
Under 21 Championships of Great Britain
The Junior Championships of Great Britain
The Junior Grass Court Championships of Great Britain
The Junior Covered Court Championships of Great Britain
Registered Coaches Championships of Great Britain
Inter-County Championships on Hard Courts

Tennis for Schools

Inter-County Championships on Grass
Junior Inter-County Championships

Lawn Tennis Performance Award Scheme

This is organised by The Lawn Tennis Professionals' Association of Great Britain, as an elementary test of skill with a certificate award. For details apply to:

Miss P. Tasker,
54 Lyndhurst Gardens,
Finchley,
London, N.3.

Organisations

The Lawn Tennis Association

Founded in 1888, with Honorary Secretaries until 1911, when the first professional Secretary was appointed and served until 1948. Mr S. Basil Reay, O.B.E. has been serving that position since then.

The L.T.A. is based on County and not regional membership, and is one of the 99 Associations affiliated to the International Lawn Tennis Federation, founded in 1913. They have 3,000 affiliated clubs and about 2,000 affiliated schools and organise the Wimbledon Championships in co-operation with the All England Tennis Club, and by legal agreement take the surplus from the Championships and use the money for the development of the game. The first Championships were actually played at Wimbledon in 1877, eleven years before the L.T.A. was founded.

They are now virtually the governing body for lawn tennis in Great Britain and publish their 'Rules of the Lawn Tennis Association' in their *Official Handbook* annually (price in 1973 – £1.50). Their headquarters address is:

The Lawn Tennis Association,
Barons Court,
London, W14 9EG.
(Telephone: 01-385 2366).

You must establish contact with them. You need their help.

The Lawn Tennis Foundation of Great Britain

Formed in 1961 to encourage more people to play the game of Lawn Tennis. It is the only full-time, non-profit-making organisation sponsoring the game, with particular emphasis on working through the large National Youth Organisations in the country.

The Foundation co-operates with the L.T.A., The Central Council of Physical Recreation, and Education Authorities and

Tennis for Schools

Parks Departments throughout Great Britain. It works closely with The Scottish L.T.A., The All-England Lawn Tennis and Croquet Club, The British Association of Organisers and Lecturers in Physical Education, The Lawn Tennis Registered Professional Coaches Association, The National Playing Fields Association, and The Physical Education Association.

Its main aim is:

1. Supplying information on HOW, WHEN and WHERE to play.
2. Assisting in setting up coaching centres for beginners.
2. Organising 'Spotlight on Lawn Tennis' Demonstrations, Tennis Rallies, Festivals, and Lawn Tennis Weeks.
4. Sponsoring events to achieve this aim.
5. Working in close association with all other organisations interested in the development of Lawn Tennis in England, Scotland, Wales and Ireland.

They are the organisers of the famous 'Nestlé National Schools Ladder Tournament' (approved by the L.T.A.) and are able and willing to offer advice and assistance with any scheme designed to promote Lawn Tennis.

They issue their 'Annual Report', with its information on clubs, competitions, coaching, and organisations across the country; and supply leaflets, pamphlets and coaching advice on request. *Lawn Tennis: Hints for Teachers on Class Coaching*, by Jack Moore, Manger of The Foundation and sponsored by Slazengers, is a practical example of their working literature. Contact them at:

The Lawn Tennis Foundation of Great Britain,
The Queen's Club,
West Kensington,
London, W14.
(Telephone: 01-385 4233/4)

United States Lawn Tennis Association

This Association matches the L.T.A. of Great Britain and covers a vast area of town and country with its governing powers for the sport. With typical American efficiency, they compile and issue an

Organisations

'Offical Publications List' annually, headed by their *Official USLTA Year Book,* and their USLTA Film List. Prices reviewed each year. They are happy to supply information on request. Contact them at:

> United States Lawn Tennis Association,
> 51 East 42nd Street,
> New York, N.Y. 10017.

The USLTA have a 'grass roots', educational programme for tennis run by—

> Mrs Eve Kraft,
> 71 University Place,
> Princeton, N.J. 08540.

Information is available on request. This could be most useful.

The Lawn Tennis Association of Australia

This is the National Association for Australia and is responsible only for the co-ordination of tennis events there, as well as dealing with ex-Australian matters and with their other National Associations for sport.

The six States of Australia each have their own Lawn Tennis Association and are members of the National body. Players, Clubs, Associations and other authorities concerned with the game, are either affiliated with or recognised by these six State L.T.A.'s. The address of the National body is:

> The Lawn Tennis Association of Australia,
> 128 Jolimont Road,
> East Melbourne 3002.

Their six State addresses are:

> N.S.W.L.T.A., 30 Alma Street, Paddington, N.S.W. 2021
> L.T.A.S.A., 47 Greenhill Road, Wayville, S.A. 5034
> L.T.A.V., Glenferrie Road, Kooyong, Vic. 3144
> Q.L.T.A., G.P.O. Box 2027, Brisbane, Q'ld. 4001
> T.L.T.A., G.P.O. Box 155B, Hobart, Tas. 7001
> W.A.L.T.A., P.O. Box 138, West Perth, WA. 6005

Tennis for Schools

With this 'International Quartet' for tennis, we encompass the globe. I wasn't going to pretend to have the ability to offer information on all the tennis associations of the world, so I'm taking this short cut. One consolation: if you should want information from other countries, at least there is a starting point of sorts here. And as I said before, these four are very willing to help. Back in Britain, there are some more organisations with whom it would pay you to make contact, like these:

The Girls' Schools Lawn Tennis Association

Hon. Sec., Miss M. E. Parker,
'Cobblers',
East Shalford Lane,
Guildford,
Surrey.

It has been formed over twenty years now and is affiliated to the L.T.A. Its purpose is to help raise the standard of tennis in girls' schools by holding teachers' courses, schoolgirl holiday courses, and by publishing termly bulletins with tennis information. This includes articles on play and practice, notices of new films and books, competitions for school members, dates of junior tournaments and the results of school girls' tournaments.

Membership is open to all Secondary Schools with an entry fee of only 13p and an annual subscription of 50p per school per annum.

The Boys' Schools Lawn Tennis Association

Hon. Secretary/Treasurer:
W. E. Curtis,
50 Royal Hospital School,
Ipswich, Suffolk IP9 2RT.

This is the counterpart of the Girls' Association and between them they are able to offer a valuable service for the advancement of tennis in schools.

Organisations

AIMS

To encourage an interest in lawn Tennis in boys' schools of all types. To create opportunities for competitive play, coaching and training courses for boys from member schools.
To act as liaison with the L.T.A., the governing body of Tennis.

REGULAR NATIONAL EVENTS

CHAMPIONSHIPS at the All England Club, Wimbledon, in mid-July. School terms of two players play singles with a deciding doubles if required.
Trophies Under 19, Clark Cup. *Plate*, Ramsden Cup.
Trophies Under 15.4, Milbourn Cup. *Plate*, Cheetham Cup.
Residential accommodation is available.

COACHING

RESIDENTIAL COACHING COURSES for schoolboys in the Easter school holidays. Courses held at the National Recreation Centres at the Crystal Palace, Lilleshall Hall, Shropshire and Bisham Abbey, Marlow, Bucks., for Senior School team players.
RESIDENTIAL TRAINING COURSE for schoomasters at Crystal Palace. Held in January each year. Coaching methods, practices and ideas.
B.S.L.T.A. NATIONAL COACH: Dudley Georgeson. Other coaches from the Georgeson School of lawn Tennis.

REGIONAL EVENTS

B.S.L.T.A. Regions – North, East, South West, Midlands, South and Home Counties North. Each with its own secretary and committee.
Tournaments for boys under 19, 16 and 14 years in each region. For School terms of two, mainly playing singles.
Coaching Courses. Residential and non-residential courses for the younger players.

Tennis for Schools

INTER-REGIONAL TOURNAMENT

The Regional winners play at Wimbledon in July for the Inter-regional Trophies.

PUBLICATIONS

Bulletins to schools in October and January. A Handbook to be issued in May, starting in 1974.

AWARDS

B.S.L.T.A. recommends the Lawn Tennis Professional's Award Scheme, which is organised for the L.T.P. Association by Miss Pauline Tasker, c/o the Georgeson School of Lawn Tennis.
Hon Tournaments Secretary B.S.L.T.A., J. R. Coates, 11, Train Avenue, Beverley High Road, Hull, Yorks.

Other organisation for tennis in Britain

SCOTTISH L.T.A.
Secretary: D. Manson,
1 Royal Terrace,
Edinburgh, EH7 5AD.

IRISH L.T.A. (ULSTER COUNCIL)
Dr J. O. Darbyshire, M.A.,
4 Glen Road,
Jordanstown,
Newtown Abbey,
Co. Antrim.

TENNIS & RACKETS ASSOCIATION
Jt. Hon. Secs:
Col. N. S. Renny, O.B.E.,
Ashley Court South,
Ashstead,
Surrey.

WELSH L.T.A.
Hon. Sec.: W. F. Cole, A.F.I.B.,
The Chimes,
Heol-y-Bryn,
Barry,
Glamorgan.

L.T.A. REGISTERED PROFESSIONAL
COACHES ASSOCIATION
Hon. Sec.: E. Garfield Hughes,
9 Suffolk Road,
The Avenue,
Worcester Park,
Surrey.

J. R. Greenwood, J.P.,
Stonehall,
Bothcombe,
Sussex.

Organisations

INTERNATIONAL LAWN TENNIS FEDERATION
Jt. Hon. Secs.:

Mr S. B. Reay, O.B.E.,
The International Lawn Tennis Federation,
Barons Court,
West Kensington,
London, W14 9EG.

Mr B. Berthet,
Federation Internationale de Lawn-Tennis,
15 rue de Teheran,
Paris 75008.

IRISH L.T.A.
Hon. Sec., Mr C. Brennan,
15 Cilleanna,
Raheny,
Dublin 5.

THE UNIVERSITY LAWN TENNIS CLUBS
Hon. Sec., R. W. Drysdale,
Oriel College, Oxford,
Hon. Sec., K. B. McCollum,
Downing College, Cambridge.

These additional two Commonwealth Associations should be useful to keep with the main pool of organisations on our list – there is, after all, considerable two-way communication.

CANADIAN L.T.A.
Secretary: B. O'Brien,
Canadian L.T.A.,
Sports Admin. Centre,
333 River Road,
Vanier City,
Ontario, KIL 8B9.

NEW ZEALAND L.T.A.
The Secretary,
New Zealand L.T.A.
G.P.O. BOX 1645,
Wellington, C.I.

I'm closing the list, as it were, at this stage. If you do obtain the 'Official Handbook' of the L.T.A., I'm sure you'll be delighted at the scrupulously prepared information linking you up with the world of tennis.

Finally, any book on sport, physical education and recreation, would be incomplete without a link-up with these two British organisations:

THE PHYSICAL EDUCATION ASSOCIATION OF GREAT BRITAIN AND NORTHERN IRELAND

A non-Governmental body, originally founded as the Ling Physical Education Association in 1899. Its main object is to

Tennis for Schools

encourage and promote the scientific study of physical health in the community, through physical and health education and recreation.

It attains this objective by – *research, publications, meetings, information and advisory service, reference and lending library, lecture service,* and extensive, up-to-date *book department,* for purchase or loan.

Membership by annual subscription. Enquiries (with s.a.e.) to: General Secretary, The Physical Education Association, Ling House, 10 Nottingham Place, London, W1M 4AX. (Telephone: 01-486 1301/2)

It is recommended that all teachers should support this national professional organisation.

THE SPORTS COUNCIL

The old lovable C.C.P.R. with a face-lift and more government backing. They operate from National Headquarters at 26 Park Crescent, London W1N 4AJ. (Telephone: 01-580 6822-9) and publish a quarterly *Sport & Recreation* magazine and *Sports Development Bulletin*. They want action from the public for more people to follow their instinct to play and participate in sport and recreation through their 'Sport for All' campaign, operated by local authorities, regional sports councils, voluntary groups and governing bodies of sport. Coaching courses include popular 'Family' weeks and 'Holiday Community' courses; plus festivals, conferences, demonstrations and exhibitions. Member subscription is currently £1.00 a year from each September 1st.

Further Reading and Teaching Material

Books for school or home
British Books

The Lawn Tennis Association Official Handbook (annually) from the L.T.A., Baron's Court, West Kensington, London, W14 9EG. £1.50 (including postage).

Improving Your Tennis by C. M. Jones. Faber and Faber Ltd., 3 Queen Square, London, WC1. 1973. £1.75 plus 12p p & p.

Better Tennis by Harry Hopman. Kaye & Ward, London. 1972. £1.15.

Lawn Tennis Group Coaching by the Girls' Schools L.T.A., from Miss M. E. Parker, 'Cobblers', East Shalford Lane, Shalford, Guildford, Surrey. 3rd. edition revised. 15p.

Aids to Tennis Teaching by W. G. Moss. From the Secretary, Scottish Lawn Tennis Association, 1 Royal Terrace, Edinburgh, EH7 5AD. (Up to date) 25p.

A Tennis Professional's Notebook, Tennis Practice and Exercises, and *Tactics for Tennis*. All three by Dudley Georgeson. From 54 Lyndhurst Gardens, Finchley, London, N.3. 20p each.

Lawn Tennis – Know the Game Series. Obtainable from Educational Productions Ltd., East Ardsley, Wakefield, Yorkshire. 20p (including postage).

Improve Your Tennis by Tony Mottram. A Penguin Handbook. 40p.

Lawn Tennis by Jack Moore. Weidenfield & Nicholson Ltd., 164 Oxford Street, London, W.1. 62½p.

Lawn Tennis: magazine – official journal of the L.T.A. published monthly, 15p. booksellers. £2 annual subscription from Lawn Tennis Ltd., 'Lowlands', Wenhaston, Halesworth, Suffolk.

Tennis for Schools

Tennis World: magazine – from Tennis World Ltd., Lancaster Road, Hinckley, Leicestershire. Single copy 20p. plus postage. Ten issues a year, £2 post paid.

World of Tennis yearbook, sponsored jointly by the BP International Tennis Fellowship and the Commercial Union Grand Prix. Published by Queen Anne Press, London, as a valuable guide to the current world game, giving all the facts and figures of the immediate season.

Lawn Tennis Competitions for Schools Compiled and edited by J. G. Rae. Obtainable only direct from J. G. Rae, 91 Buncer Lane, Blackburn Lancs., BB2 6SN. 10p (including postage).

Here is everything one needs to know about competitions organized for schools by the L.T.A., The Boys' and Girls' Schools Associations, the Public Schools L.T.A., The Nestlé and the Queen's Club Schoolgirls' Tournaments.

American Books

The United States Lawn Tennis Association issue an *Official Publications List* upon request, from: ULSTA Publications, 71 University Place, Princeton, New Jersey 08540, U.S.A. Here are some titles to consider:

1973 Official USLTA Year Book,	$4.00
Tennis Group Instruction Manual by USLTA-AAHPER, ...	$2.00
Tennis Workbooks by Eve Kraft and John Conroy:	
Unit 1 – *For Beginners and Advanced Beginners,*	$1.95
Unit 2 – *For Intermediate and Advanced Players,*	$2.95
Unit 3 – *Teacher's Guide to Group Tennis Instruction,*	$2.95
Tennis for the Coach, Teacher and Player by Harry Fogleman,	$2.50
Manual for School Tennis (mimeo),	$1.00
Ideas for Tennis Instruction – *Techniques and teaching methods,*	$1.00
Sports Illustrated Book of Tennis,	$1.95
Racket Work – *The Key to Tennis* by John M. Barnaby,	$7.95
Ed Faulkner's Tennis: How to Play it, How to Teach it,	$7.95

Further Reading and Teaching Material

Additionally, the following two titles, both very readable, are obtainable direct in the U.K.—

Getting Started in Tennis and *Advanced Tennis* by Paul Metzler. (Sterling Publishing Co. Inc., 419 Park Avenue South, New York, N.Y. 10016. Distributed in U.K. by Ward Lock Ltd., 116 Baker Street, London, W.1. 1972. £1.50).

American Magazines

Tennis USA,
Mr Bob Storer,
420 Lexington Ave.,
Room 2540,
New York, N.Y.
10017.

Tennis Magazine,
297 Westport Ave.,
Norwalk, Conn.,
06856.

World Tennis,
Mrs Gladys Heldman,
8100 Westglen,
Houston, Texas 77042

NOTE: These two British and American lists are a fair, practical selection of books most likely to be directly useful for our purpose in the context of this book on teaching and learning. In fact, they represent the best we can get at this time. But of course, we know there are dozens of tennis books on the market, many produced as 'popular' titles under the names of top world tennis stars. These kind are not so useful for our purpose, just now. We can always relax and enjoy books to widen our reading for general interest, when we've pushed ahead with the chief subject in hand, which is teaching, instructing, coaching – and of course, continuing to learn.

Pamphlets

Rules of Lawn Tennis, an official L.T.A. publication. Price 10p plus postage (3p for one copy). Obtainable from – L.T.A. Barons Court, West Kensington, London, W14 9EG.

A Precis of Lawn Tennis History published by Lawn Tennis Ltd., 'Lowlands', Wenhaston, Haleworth, Suffolk. Price 28p post free.

A Beginner's Guide to the Game of Lawn Tennis, produced by the Lawn Tennis Foundation of Gt. Britain, in co-operation with

Tennis for Schools

the Lawn Tennis Association. Obtainable from – The Lawn Tennis Foundation, The Queen's Club, West Kensington, London, W14.

Charts

Lawn Tennis Coaching Charts in colour, obtainable from – Educational Foundations Ltd., East Ardsley, Wakefield, Yorkshire. Price 35p.

Tennis Strokes: demonstrated by Ken Rosewall. Obtainable from – Lawn Tennis Foundation, The Queen's Club, West Kensington, London, W14. Price 18p. Including postage.

Film Loops

Lawn Tennis Film Loops, 1968 (series officially approved by the L.T.A.). *Lawn Tennis: Basic Stroke Play*. Obtainable from – The Loop Film Marketing Manager, MacMillan & Co. Ltd., 4 Little Essex Street, London, W.C.2.

Seven film loops devised by Dan Maskell, Training Manager of the L.T.A., especially for coaching of young people:

No. 1 Ball Sense
No. 2 Use of Racket Head
No. 3 Forehand Drive
No. 4 Backhand Drive
No. 5 Service
No. 6 Forehand and Backhand Volley
No. 7 Smash

Teaching notes supplied with each loop, which come in cassette form to fit the I.C.E.M. Standard 8 mm Daylight Projector and the Technicolour range of standard 8 mm projectors. Average running time $3\frac{3}{4}$ minutes each. Price £3.75 each.

Lawn Tennis Film Loops, 1957. (Recommended by the L.T.A. Coaches Committee). Obtainable from – Mr Guy Butler, Harbledown, Little Hadham, Hertfordshire. Price £2.10. Post paid in U.K.

Lawn Tennis Training Film Loops (approved by the L.T.A.). Obtainable from – Educational Productions Ltd., East Ardsley, Wakefield, Yorkshire. Price £5.25.

Further Reading and Teaching Material

Films on loan or for purchase

THE EDUCATIONAL FOUNDATION FOR VISUAL AIDS

No. 1 Introduction and Ball Sense (12 minutes)
No. 2 Starting to Play (14 minutes)
No. 3 The Service (9 minutes)
No. 4 Court Positions and net Play (8 minutes)

Made for The Educational Foundation for Visual Aids with the co-operation of Slazengers Ltd., and recommended by the L.T.A. Coaches Committee. Technical Adviser – Dan Maskell (Training Manager, L.T.A.)

Obtainable from your Local Education Authority or, if in difficulty, please contact: The Educational Foundation for Visual Aids, 33 Queen Anne Street, London W.1.

Each film has a booklet with teaching notes, i.e. spoken commentary. Sound. Colour. Projection speed 24 f.p.s.

TOWN AND COUNTRY PRODUCTIONS LTD

No. 1 The Way to Wimbledon
No. 2 The Way to Wimbledon (20 minutes)
No. 3 The Way to Wimbledon (16 mm Sound)

Applications should be made to Town and Country Productions Ltd., 21 Cheyne Row, Chelsea, London, S.W.3.

Booking fees – £1 (each) for one day's use; additional screenings 75p (each) per day where they are immediately subsequent to the first booking date.

Purchase price – £30.25; less 10 per cent to affiliated L.T.A. clubs and Local Education Authorities.

Films on loan

DUNLOP SPORTS CO. LTD.

Strokes for Better Tennis (20 minutes) 16 mm. Sound. Featuring Tony Mottram. Commentary by Max Robertson. Colour).

Apply to Sound Services Film Library, Kingston Road, Merton Park, London, S.W.19. No charge for hire.

Tennis for Schools

WILSON SPORTING GOOODS CO. LTD.

How to Play Tennis (25 minutes) 16 mm. Sound. Technicolour.
Apply to the Film Department, Wilson Sporting Goods Co. Ltd. Eagle House, High Street, Wimbledon, S.W.19. No charge for hire.

NOTE: SOUND FILMS CAN ONLY BE SHOWN ON SOUND MACHINES AND MUST NEVER BE SHOWN ON SILENT PROJECTORS OR THE FILM MAY BE RUINED. A SILENT FILM, ON THE OTHER HAND, MAY USUALLY BE SHOWN ON A SOUND PROJECTOR.

The foregoing deals with tennis straight. But in our over-all context where various factors of body use influence tennis performance generally, it is wise to widen our concept in terms of physical education where it relates. These additional books can be most useful:

BIODYNAMICS

The Alexander Principle by Dr Wilfred Barlow. Victor Gollancz Ltd. 1973. £3.00. A most readable, practical and wise book on the use and mis-use of the body in everyday situations of work and play.

Choice of Habit: Poise, Free Movement and the Practical Use of the Body by Jack Vinten Fenton. MacDonald & Evans Ltd. 1973. £1.25.

The Resurrection of the Body: The Writings of F. Matthias Alexander, Selected and Introduced by Edward Maisel. Dell Publishing Co. Inc., 750 Third Avenue, New York, N.Y. 10017. 1969. First Delta printing – March 1971. $2.45.

FITNESS

Live with Harcourt Roy: a modern, realistic and practical approach to health, fitness and vitality. Thorsons Publishers, Denington Estate, London Road, Wellingborough, Northants. NN8 2RQ. 1969. £1.05.

Further Reading and Teaching Material

Physical Fitness For Schools. 1971. £2. and *Physical Fitness For Boys.* 1972. £1.90 by Harcourt Roy Pelham Books, London.

P.E. INFORMATION

The Dunlop P.E. Handbook (An A-Z of Physical Education) by Derek Green, Education Officer, Dunlop Ltd., and Don Anthony, Principal Lecturer in P.E., Avery Hill College of Education. (Education Section, Dunlop Ltd., 25 St James's Street, London SW1. 1971).

Definition of a Club (from Rules of the Lawn Tennis Association)

For the purposes of these Rules, a Club is:

(a) An organisation of not less than 20 persons, of whom at least ten are of the age of 18 years or over, associated together for the purpose (either solely or inter alia) of playing lawn tennis, and managed by a committee in accordance with rules which shall be approved by the National and County Associations and if required, by the Council, and which shall provide:
   (i) For the holding of annual and other general meetings of the club;
   (ii) For the election by members of the club, either annually or at other stated periods, of their representatives on a committee of management provided that, where the ownership of the club is not vested in the members as a whole, such representation is not less than one-half of the committee; and
   (iii) For the election of officers and alteration of the rules of the club by members of the club in general meeting, or by the committee of management.

(b) A league or other organisation representing not less than 60 persons associated together for the sole purpose of playing Lawn Tennis in public parks and open spaces, and having rules approved by its National or County Association and if required, by the Council.

Definition of other affiliated organisations

For the purposes of these Rules, the expression 'other organisation' includes (a) such educational establishments as are not affiiliated as Clubs; (b) Tournament Committees; (c) Junior

Definition of a Club

Clubs; and (d) Schools. Such organisations shall not be entitled to exercise the rights conferred upon Clubs by Rules 13, 15, 18, 20 and 22 nor shall they be liable for any players' contributions under Rule 9.

Most schools have Tennis Clubs. This is a logical development of their P.E. programme – an additional motivation. In this respect, it is useful to have the 'Definition of a Club' as set out by the national governing body – The Lawn Tennis Association of Great Britain. Their 'Rules' 38 and 39 give us this information. It gives us also, a feeling of completeness, even fulfilment.

Late News Flash! The L.T.A. Green Shield Grass Roots Coaching Scheme

Objective: to provide every youngster in Great Britain with the opportunity to play tennis.

Method: six lessons of one hour each, for boys and girls at open coaching centres, by an L.T.A. Elementary Teacher or Assistant Coach for a fee of 75p. These centres can be operated at any tennis club, public park or school with one or more courts.

Operation: posters and application forms are distributed nationwide in February and March via schools, youth clubs, tennis clubs and libraries. Letters are also mailed to head teachers encouraging them to promote the scheme with their children.

Applicants are then given the time and details of the open coaching centre which they will attend.

From 2,000 children and 50 centres in 1970 when the scheme started, it has progressed to about 600 centres and 30,000 pupils in 1973 throughout Britain, with the overall responsibility with the L.T.A.s Development and Training Committee.

This scheme offers enormous benefits to the youth of any county which has an organisation interested in promoting tennis for children. And it's still expanding: there's nothing exclusive about this, it's for all the children in the land. Just get in contact with: *The Lawn Tennis Association, Barons Court, West Kensington, London, W14 9EG* (Telephone: 01-385 2366).

BP International Tennis Fellowship

Most teachers are convinced that competition is the chief motivation for sports action. So it seems that the BP International Tennis Fellowship can be a very useful support in the structure of any school's tennis programme. It was formed on 1st July 1968 to encourage Britain's best juniors and young international players with these categories of membership:

Junior Members (under 21, who have been singles winners of official tournaments under the L.T.A.). Membership lets them join in many organised activities run by the Fellowship, such as training and practice programmes, playing clinics by international coaches and national tournaments. This is the most important category for keen tennis players at school and applications arrive steadily. A very good incentive for youngsters who need to feel that someone cares about them and their tennis ability. It helps to keep them keen on training and playing – seriously.
Junior Girls Squad (under 21) selected on the strength of their performance and potential, with the opportunity to earn £100 each on their season's performance.
Junior International Members (under 21), also offered £100 on individual performance as a bonus scheme. This is a special category of British Junior Davis Cup players supported by the Fellowship.
International Members: offered an income on their results in tournaments and matches in season. This is a bonus incentive scheme open to members of the British Davis Cup squad, also sponsored by the Fellowship.
Instructional Playing Clinics: run by top professional advisers, Rod Laver and Ken Rosewall, still prominent on the international players' circuit. Tennis teachers in schools will recognise the value of these professional instructional and coaching clinics, as an incentive for pupils to improve their tennis during vacations and after-school times under expert tuition backed by enormous playing experience.

Tennis for Schools

World of Tennis – a BP Year Book published every Spring, now established as a standard reference work of the game and an aid to everyone associated with tennis – players, officials, commentators, writers or spectators.

This terrific tennis fellowship scheme has now spread to Australia, South Africa and France, and playing clinics organised in Turkey, Lebanon, Iran and Spain. It's obviously not going to stop there, and is probably the sort of motivation calculated to influence young entrants to the game and keep them on a top level of performance – *after they have proved* they are willing to seriously help themselves to start with. This is the crux, but not a puzzle: the Fellowship only accepts members who have started competitive tennis with success. It's basically a self-improvement scheme. Contact them at: BP International Tennis Fellowship, P.O. Box 10, Wimbledon, London, SW19 5AP. (Telephone: 01-684 3646).

Competence or competitiveness?

There is no resting easy until this final point is put for deliberation. Many games teachers are convinced that the best motivation to keep their pupils learning and training, is to offer them realistic competition, with the emphasis on scoring goals or winning points.

This is expected to appeal to their competitive instinct, encourage them to feel that their learning effort is worthwhile and persuade them to train hard. Presumably, this should bring talent to the top, strain off the cream and direct the really skilled performers to the tournaments and commercial circuits.

What happens to the vast majority who fail to make the tournament grade, but nevertheless still have a sizeable capacity for enjoying tennis – at their level?

On the other hand, supposing the tennis coach insisted that all his pupils be given a thorough grounding in skill-training, and they should strive conscientiously for *competence* in racket-handling and ball-sense? This coach may believe that sound stroke production is of greater value in the long run than early pre-occupation with scoring points (known as being competitive orientated).

If this good quality stroke production is conveyed with enthusiasm and efficiency, surely it can be the source of much fun and enjoyment – just as getting stimulated and involved in who is scoring and winning?

It is considered that the greater the competitive pressure in sport, the greater the psychological problems. Pushing these scoring and winning pressures too early in tennis development, may not only create psychological problems, but also cause a player to limit himself to a few select 'safe' shots in his over-concentration on winning – 'playing it safe'.

There is a connection here with the sort of person known as an 'End-gainer' in biodynamic terms, who is always scrapping to get things done, but never allows sufficient time or thought to how such jobs should be performed with the utmost efficiency and the minimum of stress. Perhaps there would be this 'End-gaining' pressure to win, for example, in a match.

To perform in such a stress-free, efficient way, however, a person would need to be aware of his own body in action and to understand the interaction of those biodynamic forces that are responsible for either grace, harmony and beauty in posture and movement, or conversely, what causes friction, stress and ugliness. He would need to understand 'the means whereby'.

To offset this possible hazard of 'End-gaining' in a competitive orientated situation, a player needs to have the solid security and confidence of a *competence* orientated development right from the beginning, or learner stage. Such a person would be more likely to command and use a much greater variety of skilful shots, played with deadly precision and devastating cool.

Players with this upbringing have made the grade to the top, like Billie Jean King, Maureen Connolly, Ken Rosewall, Rod Laver and John Newcombe.

So it's worth considering this final summing-up when it comes to deciding how the teacher's energy and talent shall be used:

When players are developed in a *competence orientated* situation, they reach a higher standard of skill and are less likely to decline, than if they had been influenced by preoccupation with a competitive orientated upbringing.

Index

Abdominal-pelvic relationship, 25
'Action feed-back', 46
Activities, 142–4
Agility, 167–70
Anchor, 77, 83, 84
Atrophy of disuse, 28
Attacking stroke, 62, 76, 77, 84
Australian L.T.A., 205
Awards, 202, 208

Backhand, 60, 66, 75, 80–6, 102, 109, 110
Backhand smash, 102
'Back-scratcher', 91–4, 95, 101
Backspin, 112
Back swing, 76, 80–3, 94
Balance, 63
Balanced resting state, 32, 71
Balls, 40, 41, 179
Ball sense, 151–2, 223
Basic body-training, 172
Basics, 63, 64
Bats, 160–2
Beginners' service, 87
Bending, 29
Big muscle activity, 171–2
Biodynamics, 23, 24, 25, 28, 30, 31, 32, 71, 72, 122, 216, 223–4
Block, 60, 104, 157
Body-awareness, 168
Body-shape, 24
Boredom factor, 50
Boys' Schools L.T.A., 197–8, 206–8
BP International Fellowship, 221–2
BP Year Book, 222
British Championships, 201–2

Canadian L.T.A., 209
'Cannon-ball', 92, 97–99
Cardiovascular fitness, 164–71, 173–4
Carpet jogging, 170, 173
'Centre Control', 25, 28, 31

C.C.P.R., 210
Charts, 214
'Chopper', 67, 68, 92, 94, 95, 100, 104
Clean-up stroke, 61–2
Clothing, 41
Competence, 223–4
Competitions, 194
Competitiveness, 223–4
Convenience shots, 120
Court measurements, 35
Cut, chop, chip, 61, 119–21

Daily maintenance work-out, 173
'Dan Maskell Tennis Trainer', 143, 149
Definition of a club, 218
Development, 167
Direct Teaching, 45, 182–3
Doubles game, 192–3
Drives, 153–4
Drop volley, 60, 115

End-gaining, 223–4
Equal status, 180
Equipment, 37

'Feed', 103, 109–10, 113, 117, 145–9
Feeders and strikers, 138, 143–4, 147
Fitness, 129, 138–9, 164–75, 216–7
Fitness Factors, 167
Fitness guide, 169–74
Films and loops, 214–16
Flexibility, 167–9
'Foot-Forward Principle', 25, 28, 30, 31, 32
Footwork, 57, 75, 76, 77, 78
Forehand, 60, 64, 65, 75–81, 100, 101, 104, 105
'Free Play', 45, 46
Free practice, 137–9
Further reading, 174–5, 211–17

225

Index

Girls' Schools L.T.A., 198–9, 206
Green Shield Scheme, 220
Grips, 57, 133
Grooving, 145
Groundstrokes, 153–4, 156–9
Gut, 39

Habitual errors, 46, 47
Half-volley, 60, 104, 107
Handball, 13
Head-neck relationship, 25, 31
Home-fitness training, 172–3

Instructional sequence, 132
International Championships, 201–2
International L.T.F., 209

'Keep the basin full', 27, 28, 31
Kinaesthetic sense, 46, 47, 48, 49, 71
'Kicker', 97–9

Lawn Tennis Association, 194, 203, 208–9
Lawn Tennis Foundation, 18, 34, 199–201, 203–4
Leading with the brow, 26, 30, 73, 76, 77, 107
Left-handed, 133, 145
Lesson plan, 137–41
'Loafer's Heart', 165
Lob, 60, 111–15, 154–5
Lob volley, 60
Long contact, 62, 78, 98, 99, 114 134
'Long Neck', 25, 26, 27, 31, 79, 85
Lumber curve, 27

Main arsenal, 60
Malfunctioning, 24, 46, 47
Motivation, 182–3
Motor-muscles, 24, 46, 47, 71, 82, 114
Movement distortion, 46, 47, 48
Muscle tone, 165
Muscular corset, 28
Muscular endurance, 167

Nestle Tournaments, 199–201
New Zealand L.T.A., 209
Nylon strings, 39

One-sided, 164–5, 170
Open stance, 86, 90, 91

'Options', 181–2
Organisations, 203–10
Overhead, 100

Padder tennis, 16, 33, 34, 159–62
P.E. Association, 209–10
Pelvic tilt, 27, 30
'Pendulum' swing, 92, 93
P.E. programme, 182, 219
Performance Award, 202
Personal gear, 41, 42
Physical re-education, 23
Pivot and place, 75, 76, 80, 83
Placing the ball, 89, 91, 92, 94
Plastic shields, 40
Posture, 167
Power, 79, 167–70
Practical reminders, 19, 53
Practice, 135
Practice wall, 36
'Predator stance', 11, 30, 32, 70–4, 104, 145
Pre-game clothing, 43
Primary, 33
Problems with school tennis, 34, 179–83
Publications, 208
Public Schools' L.T.A., 195–6
Punch, 60, 104, 105, 156
Push, 60
Push and pat, 87, 91
Pushing, 29
Pupil practice, 69, 74, 81, 82, 88, 92, 103, 109–13, 116–17, 121

Rackets, 37, 38, 39
Rallies, 153–4, 158
Reaching, 29
Re-action stroke, 61
'Reading the play', 47
'Ready position', 59, 70–1, 75, 80–1
Real tennis, 13
Return of service, 60
Rules of Lawn Tennis, 184–93

School P.E., 165–71
Schools' Tournaments, 196–201
Scoring, 14
Scrambling, 32, 123–7
Second spine, 28
Selection of racket, 38–9
'Self-discovery', 48–50
Service, 60, 67, 87–99, 154–5
Shadowing, 80–2, 92, 138, 145–6

Index

'Shake-hands', 64, 90, 104
'Shoulder serve', 87, 89–91
Singles game, 184–91
Skills, 169–71
Slazengers, 9, 160, 204, 215
Slice, 60, 97–9, 119–20
Smash, 60, 67, 87, 100–3, 154–5
Sports Council, 210
Stance, 57
Stop volley, 60, 116
Strength, 167–9
Stringing, 39
Strokes, 57, 58–9, 75
Swing, 60, 63, 76, 80–2, 91–4

Targets, 154–5
Teaching, 131
Teaching material, 211–17
'Tennis-court minders', 171
Tennis shoes, 41
'3 x 15' exercise theory, 172–3

Throw, 60, 87–8, 92, 95, 100
Topspin, 97–9, 111
Touch, 60–1, 111, 114
Treadmill, 159
'T.V. Bottom', 165

Underspin, 115–7
Underwear, 42
Unicorn posture, 11, 25, 26, 30, 73, 84
U.S.L.T.A., 204–5

Volley, 60, 104–10, 156–7

Watch and strike, 78, 85
Walls, 109, 110, 149, 157–9
Weakness, 165
Weight transfer, 77, 81, 84, 95, *96*

Young children, 180–1